The Mental Side of Softball for Young Female Athletes

A Complete Guide to Empowering Confidence, Mental Toughness, and Focus for Every Challenge (Interactive Workbook)

Vicky McFarland

Table of Contents

Free Gift

Thank you for your purchase! To show my appreciation, I'm offering my readers a FREE copy of *The Daily Softball Journal.*

Claim your free book instantly by visiting: vickymcfarland.com/free-gift

Here's what's inside:

- **3 pages of mental and physical trackers** designed specifically for young female athletes.
- **Daily writing prompts** to inspire meaningful journal reflections.
- **A physical tracker** to help athletes stay healthy and perform at their best.

If you're ready to elevate your game both on and off the field, don't miss this opportunity to grab your free copy!

Introduction

Welcome to a journey that's all about you! Changing how you think and feel on the softball field and beyond. Picture game day, and you're standing at the plate, the sun warming your face, gripping the bat tightly as you eye the pitcher. You hear the cheers of teammates and spectators, but there's a tiny voice inside questioning if you've got what it takes. Sound familiar? Every young athlete faces those moments of doubt, moments where confidence feels like a distant dream. But here's the secret: by mastering the mental game, you can power through with confidence and focus.

I'm thrilled to share this guide with you because I've been in your cleats. I played softball at a Division 1 college level and took my passion around the world, playing professionally in Germany, Australia, and Italy. That journey wasn't always a smooth one. As an athlete, I faced my own battles with mindset—days when negative thoughts seeped in after a missed catch or strikeout. Those were the days that truly tested my mental toughness. Fortunately, I had incredible mentors who guided me, helping shift my perspective from feeling defeated to seeing challenges as opportunities. And that's exactly why I'm here—to pass on those lessons, giving you the tools to build unshakeable confidence on and off the field.

As a coach today, I notice many young female athletes caught up in trying to perfect their physical skills but often overlook the mental side of sports. It's understandable—after all, hitting a home run is way more fun than overcoming self-doubt. But the mental game is just as important. My coaching sessions go beyond drills—we'll dive into growth mindset discussions, work on building positive self-talk, and journal our hopes and fears. This will change not just performance but also the entire experience of being on a team. So, I decided to write this book, creating a resource that goes hand-in-hand with your training to uplift your mental game.

You might be wondering, "Why does mindset matter so much?" Well, let's break it down. Mindset is like a pair of glasses through which you see both your wins and setbacks. If you're wearing lenses clouded with self-doubt, even small mistakes seem huge. But pop on a pair of growth mindset lenses, and mistakes turn into valuable lessons. It's all about seeing setbacks not as roadblocks but as building blocks. Think about it—when you're tripped up by a missed pitch, it's easy to get lost in frustration. If you switch to viewing that moment as a learning opportunity, your whole approach changes. Wouldn't it be amazing to step onto the field each time with an unwavering belief in your potential?

Imagine feeling an unshakeable sense of confidence every time you lace up your cleats. Picture yourself bouncing back from challenges stronger than ever before. This isn't wishful thinking; You can do it by building a strong mindset. With this workbook, you'll uncover strategies to help you achieve exactly that. We'll kick things off by setting specific goals that align with your dreams. Each chapter will guide you through exercises that bring mindset principles alive in practice scenarios. From reflection prompts to journaling, you'll see into your personal journey, harnessing these experiences to fuel future successes.

This is more than a guide—it's an interactive adventure packed with actionable exercises designed to apply mindset techniques in real life. Think of it as your personal playbook for tackling the mental challenges of sports. As you flip through these pages, you'll discover how to tap into confidence you didn't even know you had. The practices within these chapters will help you build lasting habits that elevate not only your performance but boost your sporting experience altogether.

My goal here is simple: To support your continuous growth and success as an athlete. I believe in empowering your self-confidence and resilience, making sure you're ready for whatever comes your way. Through stories, exercises, and reflections, you'll find real tools that fit into your daily routine, boosting your mental game alongside physical training. It is time to invest in yourself and shape a future where your mental strength matches your skill on the field.

So, are you excited to unlock your potential and create a mindset that lets you shine brightly on the field and beyond? Get ready to start on this exciting path, where each page brings you closer to unleashing your true potential. Let's dive in, equip ourselves with great confidence, tackle those fears head-on, and step boldly into the world of competitive sports.

Are you set to inspire yourself and others with your strength? Let's do this together—one page and one exercise at a time.

Chapter 1: Welcome to Your Athletic Mindset Adventure

The only one who can tell you 'you can't win' is you, and you don't have to listen. —Jessica Ennis-Hill

As you lace up your cleats and pick up your bat, there's more at play than just physical skill—it's about harnessing the power of your mind to achieve your best performance on the field. When you're part of a softball team and gearing up for a major game, each moment demands both physical prowess and mental fortitude. This chapter will guide you through how your mindset can become your best teammate. It's fascinating how much of a difference the right mindset can make in sports, from boosting confidence to improving game strategies.

In this chapter, you'll look into the intricate world of mindsets and their important role in sports. It's time to gain a better understanding of how to nurture that all-important growth mindset, setting the stage for personal and athletic success.

Growth Mindset vs. Fixed Mindset

How you approach every game impacts your performance. This is where understanding your mindset comes into play—it can be a game-changer.

What Is a Growth Mindset and Why Do I Want One?

When you have a growth mindset, you understand that your abilities aren't set in stone. Instead, they're like muscles that can grow and develop through dedication and hard work. It's important because this kind of thinking is what makes you resilient. You learn to bounce back from losses and setbacks, viewing them as opportunities rather than obstacles. This is resilience at its finest! This way of thinking encourages you to keep pushing forward, knowing that improvement is always possible at every practice and game.

Ditching a Fixed Mindset

On the flip side, there's something called a fixed mindset, which can be quite limiting. If you believe that your talents and capabilities are fixed, you might start fearing failure more than anything else. This fear can stifle your growth because every mistake feels like a final judgment on your ability. An example could be the first time you tried bunting and it went horribly wrong. If you thought, "I sucked at that, I will never bunt again," that was your fixed mindset showing you who's boss.

Instead of trying new things or pushing yourself, you might hold back, worried that any misstep means you're not good enough. And when you think about it, that's tough because making mistakes is how we all learn. In sports, especially, shying away from challenges can limit your potential and development.

Athletes with a growth mindset tend to take risks and see them as part of their journey. Now, let's say you step back up to bat with the confidence to try a new bunting technique your coach taught you. You're ready to give it a shot, even if it means striking out the first few times. With each strike, you see what works and what doesn't, gradually improving your form. If you were still stuck in a fixed mindset, you might get discouraged after that first strikeout, struggling to recover during future games.

Real-Life Example

Let's look at a real-life example of how these mindsets play out. Consider an athlete who's faced numerous defeats but kept at it due to her growth mindset.

Serena Williams, one of the greatest tennis players (winning more single Grand Slam titles than anyone) in history, stands out. She didn't win every match she played—far from it. But what sets her apart is her relentless drive to learn from every loss and continue improving her skills. At just 17, she won her first U.S. Open title. Her story is a testament to how powerful a growth mindset can be in overcoming hurdles and achieving greatness (McCoy, 2020).

On the contrary, many promising athletes with remarkable talent often plateau because they believe they are already as good as they could get. This fixed mindset limited their room for improvement, keeping them from reaching their full potential.

If you find yourself hesitating before a big play or doubting your skills after a tough practice, remember the power of shifting your perspective. Building your growth mindset can help you stay motivated and focused, regardless of the challenges you face. It's about looking at the hurdles not as roadblocks but as building blocks toward becoming the best athlete you can be.

When you adopt a growth mindset, you're more likely to experiment and innovate in your sport. Imagine learning new pitches in softball or trying different base-running strategies. Each attempt becomes a learning process, adding to your skillset over time. This flexibility helps break away from the rigidity of a fixed mindset, where the fear of failing prevents you from moving beyond your comfort zone.

Building this growth mindset doesn't happen overnight. It takes time and consistent effort. Start by setting small goals for yourself in your sport, like hitting the ball hard into play or mastering a particular drill. And when things don't go as planned, resist the urge to criticize yourself harshly. Instead, ask, "What can I learn from this?"

Why Mindset Matters in Sports

In the captivating world of sports, having a positive mindset is like wearing an invisible cape that empowers you to perform your best, especially when you're feeling the heat. Developing this mental strength can be just as important as physical training. Imagine being at bat with bases loaded and two outs. At this moment, managing stress and staying focused is key. Developing a positive mindset helps strengthen focus and shrink those anxious butterflies.

A proactive mindset involves adopting strategies like positive self-talk and visualization, which work wonders during high-pressure situations. Saying to yourself, "I can handle this," or envisioning success can make all the difference in performance. It's about seeing pressure as an opportunity to shine rather than a hurdle. By practicing these mental strategies consistently, you condition your mind to remain calm and collected even when the pressure is on.

But what happens when setbacks like injuries occur? This is where resilience muscles kick in. A resilient mindset sees failures not as stop signs but as chances to grow, remember? Take the example of a softball player who, after straining her knee, chooses to show up and learn from each game instead of dwelling on not being on the field. This mindset changed her challenge into a growth opportunity, motivating her to rehabilitate harder and smarter. Bouncing back boosts not only performance on the field but also builds character off it, teaching lessons in perseverance and determination.

Resilience also shines during recovery from injuries. Mental toughness helps maintain motivation and allows you to focus on rehabilitation goals, guaranteeing you return stronger. You should view the injury recovery as a chance to develop new skills or refine existing ones. This allows you to come back with renewed strength and confidence.

Boosting Your Team Dynamics

The influence of your mindset extends beyond personal performance to affect the entire team dynamic. Picture a teammate who's always encouraging others and spreading positivity, even when the score isn't in their favor. That kind of positivity lifts the whole team's morale and creates a supportive environment. When everyone believes in collective success, team connection strengthens, building better communication and collaboration.

On the other hand, if negativity creeps into one player's mindset, it can disrupt dynamics, leading to misunderstandings and lowered spirits for the entire team. It's crucial to understand that a team thrives when each member has a mindset of encouragement and support. Leaders within the team should use open dialogue, address conflicts positively, and promote mutual respect and trust among teammates. In essence, cultivating a positive atmosphere not only boosts individual performance but also fortifies the team's spirit and togetherness.

Long Term Success

The power of a resilient mindset doesn't stop at sports; it cascades into all walks of life. The skills learned—like handling pressure, bouncing back from setbacks, and maintaining a positive outlook—can be used for success in school, social situations, and future professional scenarios. You can apply these principles in school, achieving your academic goals with perseverance and resilience. You can handle life's challenges with the same grit and grace you exhibit on the field, paving the way for a fulfilling journey both in and out of sports.

Guidelines are important in nurturing this mindset. Welcoming challenges rather than avoiding them encourages growth. Next time you face a tough opponent or a difficult exam, see it as an exciting challenge to overcome. Being open about your weaknesses and asking for feedback can reveal paths to improvement, whether it's asking your coach what to focus on or talking strategies with teammates. Remember, fear of failure can hold you back from growth—owning it and moving forward builds resilience.

Exercise: Mindset Mastery for Young Female Athletes

Objective: Strengthen the understanding of a growth mindset, resilience, and personal accountability through interactive activities.

Part 1: Interactive Scenarios

Select one of the following scenarios and write down how you would respond to show a growth mindset:

- After losing an important game, you feel disappointed. How do you deal with this emotion, and what steps do you take to improve for the next game?

_____

_____

_____

_____

_____

_____

_____

_____

_____

_____

_____

- You get constructive criticism from your coach. Reflect on your initial response and how you can use this feedback to grow as an athlete.

_____

_____

_____

_____

_____

Part 2: Goal-Setting Challenge

- Set three specific, measurable goals for your athletic development in the next month. Consider skills you want to improve, physical conditioning, or mental focus.

  - Goal one:_____

  - Goal two:_____

  - Goal three:_____

- Now, for each goal, write one action step you will take this week to achieve it.

o   Goal one action step:

_____

_____

o   Goal two action step:

_____

_____

o   Goal three action step:

_____

_____

Part 3: Reflection and Journaling

- After completing the week of goal-setting, reflect on your experiences:

  o   What challenges did you face?

_____
_____
_____
_____
_____
_____
_____
_____
_____
_____

  o   How did you overcome them?

_____
_____
_____
_____
_____
_____
_____
_____
_____
_____

  o   What did you learn about yourself during this process?

_____

_____

_____

_____

_____

_____

_____

_____

_____

_____

- Write a journal entry summarizing your mindset journey over the past week. Include instances where you practiced self-reflection and how it helped your personal growth.

_____

_____

_____

_____

_____

_____

_____

_____

_____

_____

Bringing It Home

As we've discussed throughout the chapter, your mindset is like the secret weapon you bring to every game. Welcoming a growth mindset helps you tackle challenges with confidence and learn from each experience, whether it's nailing that swing or recovering from a mistake on the field. Remember, it's not just about physical skills; how you think can boost your performance. So, when those nerves start fluttering before you're up to bat, remind yourself of all the practice and preparation you've put in. Believe in your ability to improve and grow, no matter what happens during the game.

Think about how leaning into a positive, resilient mindset extends beyond just sports. It becomes a tool for tackling schoolwork, building strong friendships, and overcoming life's everyday hurdles. Keep setting small, achievable goals like mastering a new technique or improving your stats, and celebrate each step forward. Always keep in mind that the focus shouldn't solely be on your stats but on having fun and learning. When setbacks happen—and they will—view them as learning opportunities. Ask yourself, *"What can I gain from this experience?"* With each effort, you're not just becoming better at softball but also shaping yourself into a stronger young woman ready to face whatever comes your way. Stay focused, stay positive, and most importantly, keep believing in your potential to succeed.

Chapter 2: The Power of Positive Thinking

I don't focus on what I'm up against. I focus on my goals, and I try to ignore the rest. –Venus Williams

Positive thinking is the name of the game when you're looking to boost your performance and self-confidence on the field. Harnessing the power of your mind through techniques like positive self-talk and visualization doesn't just make you feel good; it can actually change how you play.

In this chapter, you'll explore the art of turning negative self-talk into empowering affirmations. You'll learn how acknowledging those inner doubts can actually help you overcome them, leading to stronger mental resilience.

Identifying Negative Self-Talk

Recognizing and addressing negative thought patterns is important when you want to strengthen your mental game. It's not uncommon to experience moments of doubt, especially when you're critiquing your own performance on the field. Whether it's hitting, fielding, or pitching, these internal criticisms can sap your confidence and hinder your enjoyment of the game. Remember, you're not alone in this experience.

Think about a time you might have thought, "This is impossible." That's negative self-talk showing up, and it can disguise itself in many ways. This kind of thinking doesn't just affect how you feel about your skills; it directly impacts your performance by making you more anxious and less focused. Research tells us that achieving top athletic performance requires a strong set of psychological skills alongside physical fitness (Park & Jeon, 2023). When negative thoughts creep in, they mess with that balance, upping your anxiety and reducing your ability to concentrate on what you need to do next.

Internal Dialogue Awareness

Being aware of your internal dialogue is the first step in filtering out harmful thoughts and engaging in positive mental strategies. Self-talk is essentially the conversation happening in your head. It can be something like quietly reminding yourself, "I can handle this challenge."

Becoming conscious of this dialogue allows you to turn down the volume of negative comments and turn up positive affirmations, like saying, "I'm ready to give my best today."

Research highlights the value of positive self-talk as part of a sports performance strategy. While negative self-talk may seem like a minor issue, it can actually lead to increased anxiety and distraction during competition (Park et al., 2020). Imagine trying to focus on a pitch while your mind's replaying every mistake you've made—that's the power of negative self-talk.

Do You Know Your Triggers?

Part of overcoming this is recognizing the specific triggers that lead to negative thinking. Maybe it's the pressure of a big game or remembering a past error at a crucial moment. Being aware of these triggers can prepare you better for competitive environments. When you're prepared, you're less likely to slip into negativity because you can anticipate that trigger coming and actively choose how to react to it.

When you start noticing these thoughts, it helps to write them down. Perhaps you're prone to thinking something like, "I always swing and miss when it matters." Once it's on paper, ask yourself, "Is there a more helpful way to say this?" You could reframe it to: "I've been practicing hitting, and I put a good swing on that pitch." This doesn't mean ignoring mistakes or pretending everything is perfect. Instead, it's about shifting your focus to growth and improvement, which is a much more productive mindset.

Reframing your self-talk takes deliberate practice. Whenever those old thoughts pop up, replace them with the new ones you've prepared. Speak them out loud if you can, or say them internally. Over time, with repetition, these positive statements will become your default reaction, boosting your confidence and reducing performance-related stress.

By focusing on refining these skills, you build your mental resilience, which can translate into improved performance on the field. The goal isn't to eliminate all negative thoughts but rather to recognize and manage them better.

Replacing Negative Thoughts With Positive Affirmations

In the world of softball, where performance and mental focus matter, learning to steer your thoughts toward positivity can make all the difference. Think of affirmations as mental conditioning drills that help you build a stronger, more confident self-image—much like practicing your swing until it's second nature. These positive statements are tools designed to reinforce your belief in yourself and improve how you view your abilities.

Creating Personal Affirmations and Using Them Daily

To start crafting affirmations that work for you, it's important to think about what you want to achieve on the field. Personalized affirmations tailored specifically to your needs in softball are much more effective than generic ones. Are you striving to be a quicker thinker when running bases? Try saying, "I am a smart baserunner." Or maybe you want to boost your confidence while pitching; an affirmation like "I command the mound" could resonate with you. Creating these personalized affirmations involves focusing on specific aspects of your game you wish to enhance and framing them positively.

Once you've crafted your affirmations, incorporating them into your daily routine is key. Just like any other skill, consistency is essential. Set aside time each day to practice your affirmations. This could be during morning stretches, pre-game warm-ups, or before heading to bed. Daily repetition helps solidify these positive ideas in your mind, gradually changing your mindset from negative to empowering. Over time, this practice can sharpen your focus during games, boost your confidence, and even improve your overall performance. It's similar to how regular physical training builds muscle memory and strength—your brain responds positively to these repeated affirmations by creating a greater sense of self-worth and capability.

Exercise: Reframe Your Thoughts

Write down three negative thoughts you often have during softball.

_____
_____
_____
_____
_____

Now, reframe those same thoughts in a positive light.

_____
_____
_____

How Can Affirmations Benefit You?

Beyond improving your game, maintaining a positive mindset through affirmations can help you become more resilient and emotionally balanced. Challenges and setbacks happen in sports, but having a steady reserve of positive beliefs can keep you from being overwhelmed by negativity. When things get tough, being able to flip that internal dialogue to something more reassuring can stabilize your emotions and keep you focused on your goals. Affirmations such as "I handle challenges with ease" or "I stay calm under pressure" can change how you deal with stressful situations, keeping your mind clear and composed on and off the field.

Furthermore, scientific studies support the power of affirmations in boosting mental resilience. Research points out that positive affirmations activate brain regions associated with self-worth and motivation, making them valuable tools for athletes looking to improve their mental game (Cascio et al., 2015). Practicing self-affirmation has been linked to decreased stress levels and improved problem-solving abilities, both necessary for maintaining calm during intense competition (Cascio et al., 2015).

To blend affirmations into your life, set realistic goals and track your progress. Reflect on your experiences and adjust your affirmations if necessary. As you grow and develop new skills, your affirmations should evolve, too. The purpose of affirmations isn't just to repeat positive words but to instill a lasting change in how you perceive yourself and your capabilities. With every affirmation, you plant seeds of confidence that, with time and commitment, bloom into actual improvements in your athletic and personal life.

How Visualization Helps in Sports

As said by Jennie Finch: "Before you even get on the field, imagine yourself there. Envision yourself giving it 100%. What is the end result you want? What do you want to feel when the game is over? Play for THAT moment. Guard your thoughts. Get rid of any negativity and self-doubt. Fill your mind with positive affirmations, and speak them over your teammates also! When you can master your mind, you can master the game (Finch, n.d.)."

In the world of competitive sports, visualization is a secret weapon that many young athletes overlook. It's not just about physical training; it's about preparing your mind for success, too. By simulating experiences mentally, visualization helps prime the brain to perform at its best, increasing confidence and reducing anxiety when you step onto the field (Adams, 2020). You might think that mental preparation sounds vague, but it's a technique used by elite athletes worldwide.

Think about what a pro softball player like Jennie Finch does to prepare for a game. They don't just practice their routines physically; they also spend time imagining every detail of their performance. They visualize the feel of the equipment, the sound of the crowd, even the emotions they'll experience. This process creates mental movies that make them better prepared for actual play.

As a young softball athlete, you can use these techniques, too.

Why Does Visualization Work?

But what makes visualization so effective? When paired with physical execution, this technique boosts skill retention and readiness. Think of it like this: By repeatedly visualizing a successful outcome, you're teaching your brain and body to work together seamlessly. It's like having a dress rehearsal before the big performance, except you're rehearsing in your mind. This kind of mental preparation can make all the difference, especially under pressure.

Plus, visualization increases confidence. When you've already "seen" yourself succeed in your mind, you step onto the field feeling more assured. You've lived the moment before it happens, which drops your anxiety levels. By reducing those pre-game jitters, your actual performance improves, as you're less bogged down by nerves and more focused on your strategic play.

How Do I Visualize?

To truly benefit from visualization, engage all your senses. What do you hear? Is it the crack of the bat? The roar of the crowd? Feel your muscles moving smoothly and confidently. Smell the dirt on the field or the freshness of the morning air. Using a first-person perspective allows you to deeply connect with the experience and mentally simulate real-life competition scenarios.

The key to mastering visualization is repetition. Like any other skill, it gets easier and more effective the more you do it. Think about adding short visualization exercises to your daily routine. Even five minutes a day can help reinforce positive imagery and mental patterns.

Aside from personal practice, incorporating guided visualization sessions can offer structure and variety. Consider listening to audio guides designed for athletes or working with a mental performance coach who can walk you through advanced techniques. They might suggest visualizing overcoming potential challenges, like bad weather conditions or making a comeback after falling behind.

At the core of visualization is the concept of emotional conditioning. Prepare for emotional highs and lows by imagining how you'd handle a mistake or a tough opponent. See yourself staying calm and resilient, maintaining focus no matter what comes your way. This level of mental toughness helps you stay ready to tackle any challenge, making you a more adaptable and confident athlete.

Set aside specific times to focus on your mental game, like before practice or games. Work with coaches or mental performance consultants, if possible, to tailor these practices to your individual needs and goals.

Visualization Exercise for Young Female Softball Athletes

Objective: Boost performance and mental readiness through successful visualization techniques.

Step 1: Relax and Center Yourself

- Find a quiet space where you feel comfortable.

- Sit or lie down in a relaxed position. Take deep breaths, inhaling for a count of four and exhaling for a count of four. Repeat this for a few minutes until you feel calm and focused.

Step 2: Create Your Success Scenario

- Close your eyes and imagine yourself stepping onto the field for a big game. Visualize the sights, sounds, and smells around you.

- Picture yourself going through your warm-up routine. Feel the energy in your body and the confidence building within you.

Step 3: Visualize Key Plays

- Envision a specific play you want to excel at, such as hitting a home run or making a perfect catch.

- As you visualize this play, see yourself performing it flawlessly. Imagine every detail— your stance at the plate, your swing, the ball soaring through the air, and the cheers from your teammates.

Step 4: Feel the Confidence

- As you visualize these successful moments, pay attention to the emotions you feel— pride, excitement, and confidence. Allow yourself to fully experience these positive feelings.

Step 5: Integrate Visualization into Training

- Before practice, take a few moments to visualize the skills you want to improve.

- Pair your mental practice with physical drills. For example, before batting practice, visualize the perfect swing you want to achieve.

Step 6: Pre-Game Visualization

- Before each game, set aside time to repeat this visualization process.

- Picture yourself playing at your best, focusing on how you will feel as you successfully execute your skills throughout the game.

Reflection

After finishing the exercise, take a moment to reflect:

- How did visualization make you feel?

_____

_____

- Did you notice any changes in your confidence or anxiety levels?

_____

_____

- Write down your thoughts and experiences in a journal to track your progress and growth.

Visualization is not just a technique; it's an important part of your mental game strategy. When you consistently practice visualization, you will strengthen not only your skills but also your confidence and readiness to face challenges on the field. Every great athlete visualizes their success—now it's your turn to step into that role.

Bringing It Home

We've covered a lot in this chapter, focusing on how positive self-talk and visualization can be game-changers for you. By recognizing and replacing negative thoughts with empowering affirmations, you're taking control of your mental game. This isn't just about feeling good; it's about building the confidence and focus needed to perform at your best. Whether you're visualizing hitting a tough pitch or reminding yourself that you've got what it takes, these techniques help lower your anxiety and keep you centered during competition. Remember, practice makes perfect—not just physically but mentally, too.

Incorporating these mental strategies into your routine might seem challenging at first, but consistency is key. Just like perfecting your swing or refining your fielding skills, the more you practice, the better you'll get. Make self-talk and visualization a regular part of your training, and don't hesitate to adjust them as you grow. The goal is to build a mindset that fuels your motivation and builds resilience, both on and off the field. Stay committed to this journey because, with every affirmation and visualized success, you're planting seeds for not only becoming a stronger athlete but a more confident individual.

Chapter 3: Believing in Yourself—Building Confidence

Anything worthy of your passion should be worthy of your preparation. –Sue Enquist

Believing in yourself is everything, especially when you're out on the softball field. It's not just about winning or losing; it's about developing a mindset that fuels your passion and drives your performance. See yourself stepping onto the field with confidence radiating from every pore, ready to take on any challenge that comes your way. Confidence changes everything, making each swing, pitch, and catch sharper and more precise. But how do you develop this confidence, and why does it matter so much? Understanding the impact of self-belief goes far beyond sports—it touches every part of your life.

In this chapter, we'll dive deep into what confidence truly is and how it directly influences your performance on the field. Whether you're aiming to improve your game or boost your personal growth, these tools are important to stepping up and becoming the player you've always aspired to be.

Understanding Confidence and Its Impact on Performance

Confidence is like your superpower on the softball field. It's all about believing in your ability to do well and trusting that even if things don't go exactly as planned, you're still capable of succeeding. Just think about it—there have probably been times when you stepped up to bat or took your position out on the field feeling invincible. That's confidence at work. It gives you the courage to try new plays or swing for the fences without worrying too much about what might happen if things don't work out perfectly.

This inner belief is what helps you take those calculated risks during a game. You see an opportunity and decide to go for it, whether it means trying to steal a base or attempting that diving catch. Confidence doesn't mean you're sure you'll get it right every time, but it lets you move forward even with uncertainty. That's a powerful thing because sports are all about taking chances and making decisions in the moment. And having that trust in yourself can make those choices easier and more effective.

How to Build Confidence

Building this confidence isn't something that just happens overnight. You've likely heard the saying that practice makes perfect, and there's truth in that when it comes to confidence. One way to boost your self-belief is by simply putting in the hours on the field. Each time you practice hitting, fielding, or pitching, you're not only sharpening your skills but also reinforcing the idea in your mind that "I can do this." Every drill you complete successfully adds another layer of confidence.

Preparation = Confidence

To really harness this, trust in your training. Remember all those early mornings, late nights, and countless drills? Those are the moments that lay the groundwork for confidence. When you're standing on the field during a key game moment, let that preparation guide you. Think back to that time you nailed a similar play in practice and channel that energy. Trusting your training allows you to perform knowing that you've done this before and you can do it again.

In fact, focusing on your training can help you stay steady under pressure. The confidence earned through preparation doesn't just disappear in high-stakes situations. Instead, it provides a solid foundation that can keep you grounded. Imagine being caught in a tight spot during a game—a situation you've drilled countless times in practice. In these moments, remind yourself of the effort and determination you've put into your preparation. This reassurance can allow you to focus more and make clear-headed decisions.

Confidence is not just about feeling good; it actually affects how well you play. With higher levels of confidence, you'll likely notice improvements in your focus and concentration. It clears your mind of doubts and worries, allowing you to concentrate fully on the task at hand. Picture yourself at the plate, blocking out any distractions and zeroing in on the pitch with laser-like focus. Your confidence keeps your thoughts positive and your attention where it belongs—on executing the play. If you aren't feeling confident in your own preparation, you need to put in the work outside of practice hours to build that confidence.

A big takeaway is that confidence breeds resilience. Sometimes, games won't go your way, or you'll make mistakes—we all do. But if you're confident, bouncing back from setbacks becomes much easier. Instead of dwelling on a missed catch or strikeout, you remind yourself of the times you've succeeded and use that to push forward. Resilience, powered by confidence, makes you more adaptable and better equipped to turn things around after a less-than-perfect play.

Link Between Confidence and Performance

Research shows that athletes who possess higher self-confidence are more likely to achieve better results (Jekauc et al., 2023). This confidence can come from many sources such as training, positive reinforcement, and overcoming challenges. Plenty of successful female athletes regard confidence as a central factor in their achievements.

To illustrate this point, we can look at the story of a prominent young female athlete:

- **Mo'ne Davis:** Gaining fame in 2014 after leading her team to the Little League World Series at the age of 13, Mo'ne Davis showcased remarkable confidence on the mound. Despite being the first girl to earn a win in the tournament's history, she faced overwhelming pressure. Mo'ne's confidence in her abilities allowed her to perform at her best, inspiring countless young athletes. She overcame the challenge of being in the spotlight by focusing on her skills and passion for the game (Sutelan, 2024).

And let's not forget Dot Richardson, a pioneer in women's sports. Dot had an illustrious athletic career as a two-time Olympic gold medalist in softball and a celebrated physician. Throughout her journey, her confidence was a driving force. She faced challenges such as balancing her medical career with athletics and competing against a landscape that often undervalued women's sports. Dot's self-assured demeanor and unwavering belief in her capabilities allowed her to excel on the world stage. Her resilience and confidence not only led to personal success but also helped pave the way for future generations of female athletes (McCoy, 2020).

Confidence also impacts physiological responses, like heart rate and stress levels, which can greatly influence performance. Athletes with high confidence levels often experience lower stress, leading to better decision-making and enhanced physical execution during critical moments. On the other hand, a lack of confidence can result in increased anxiety, which can hinder performance (Jekauc et al., 2023).

Confidence is a mental attribute you can use beyond being a softball athlete. You can also use it to shape your physical performance and overall success in life. By learning from influential figures like Mo'ne Davis and Dot Richardson, you can understand the importance of believing in yourself and overcoming challenges on your path to greatness.

Recognizing Your Strengths and Abilities

To believe in yourself as a young female softball player, it's crucial to focus on self-awareness and understand your unique strengths. By doing this, you can boost your performance and overall confidence. Let's break down some ideas that can help you harness these strengths effectively.

Self-Assessment of Strengths

First—self-assessment is key. Have you ever taken a moment to think about what you're really good at in softball? Maybe you're great at pitching or have a knack for catching those tricky fly balls. When you identify these strengths, it's like you're setting the stage for success. This self-awareness helps you set realistic goals tailored to your abilities. For instance, if you know you're fast on your feet, try focusing on improving your base-stealing technique.

Understanding your strengths not only inspires you but also gives you a clear path to follow. It's like having a map for your journey in sports. Knowing where your skills lie allows you to aim high without setting yourself up for unrealistic expectations.

Emphasizing these strengths empowers you in many ways. Think about it—when you know what you're good at, you can use that knowledge to stand out in your specific role on the team. If you shine as a batter, own it. Take extra time to practice and refine that skill. The more you zone in on your strengths, the more you'll excel in your position. This increases your sense of competence and makes you an invaluable part of the team.

Identifying your strengths is also essential for building a positive self-image. It's easy to get caught up in comparing yourself to others, especially when you're surrounded by talented teammates. Instead, focus on what makes you unique. Recognizing your abilities reduces self-doubt and builds a stronger mental foundation. You'll carry this positivity into games and practices, resulting in better overall well-being and performance.

Exercise: Strengths Self-Assessment for Softball Athletes

Objective: To help you identify your personal strengths and understand how they can inspire confidence and empower you in your sport.

Instructions:

- **Reflection**

  - Find a quiet space where you can think without distractions.

  - Take a few deep breaths to relax.

  - Reflect on your experiences in softball. Consider the following questions:

    - What do you enjoy most about playing softball?

_____
_____
_____
_____
_____
_____
_____
_____
_____
_____

■ What do your coaches or teammates often compliment you on?

_____
_____
_____
_____

■ Think about memorable moments when you felt proud of your performance. What did you do well in those moments?

_____
_____
_____
_____

- **Strengths list**

  ○ Write "My Strengths" in the circle provided.

  ○ Around the circle, write down at least five personal strengths related to your performance in softball. These can be physical skills like speed, bunting, or throwing accuracy; mental strengths like focus, determination, or teamwork; or personal qualities like leadership, positivity, or resilience.

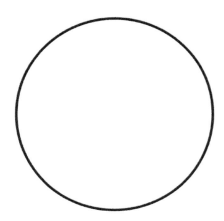

- **Goal setting**

  - Look at your list of strengths and think about how they can help you set realistic goals in your softball journey.

  - Choose one or two strengths you want to focus on improving further.

  - Write down a specific goal for each strength. For example:

    - "I want to improve my speed by practicing sprinting drills twice a week."

    - "I will work on my leadership skills by helping younger teammates during practice."

_____
_____
_____
_____
_____
_____
_____
_____
_____
_____

- **Empowerment reflection**

- ○ Reflect on how understanding your strengths influences your self-image and reduces self-doubt.

- ○ Write a short paragraph about how you will use your strengths to overcome challenges in your sport. For example: "When I face tough games, I will remind myself of my strong communication skills to keep my team motivated."

_____
_____
_____
_____
_____
_____
_____
_____
_____

- **Share and support**

  - ○ If you feel comfortable, share your strengths and goals with a teammate, coach, or family member. Encourage them to do the same.

  - ○ Support each other by checking in on your progress towards your goals.

Understanding your strengths not only boosts your confidence but also empowers you to excel in softball. Remember, celebrating what you do best sets a positive foundation for growth and success!

Reflection on Past Successes

A positive self-image is contagious, too. As you become more confident in your abilities, you'll notice a shift in how you view challenges. No longer filled with doubt, you'll approach tasks with determination and a fresh outlook. This mindset benefits not only you but your entire team as they feed off your energy and determination.

Knowing what you're capable of encourages ownership of your achievements. It's important to recognize when you've done something amazing, whether it's nailing that home run or making a crucial catch. Taking ownership allows you to internalize your successes and build on them. Acknowledge your hard work and dedication—it's what propels you toward even greater accomplishments.

Owning your achievements also means learning to handle setbacks gracefully. Sometimes, things don't go as planned in sports, and that's okay. What's important is reflecting on these moments and understanding what they teach you about your strengths. When setbacks occur, take a step back, reassess, and plan your next move confidently. This reflection will prepare you for future challenges and enhance your resilience.

Setting Strength-Focused Goals

To set yourself up for further success, establish realistic, achievable goals based on the strengths you've identified. Start small, focusing on areas you know you excel in, then gradually expand your efforts. Track your progress, celebrate your wins, and adjust your approach as needed. Setting objectives keeps you motivated, provides direction, and instills a sense of purpose.

Finally, having an open dialogue with your coach and teammates about your strengths can be incredibly beneficial. Share your insights and listen to their feedback—it might reveal additional strengths you hadn't considered. Collaborating with others reinforces your confidence and builds a supportive environment that nurtures everyone's growth.

Our Body Language and Facial Expressions Speak Volumes

Let's dive into how showing up with confidence can skyrocket your game and make you feel like a true powerhouse on the field.

The Importance of Body Language

First, let's talk about positive body language. It might not sound like a big deal, but how you carry yourself can seriously change the way you feel—and how others perceive you. Picture this: you're walking onto the field with your shoulders back, head held high, and giving a confident smile. That's going to have your teammates buzzing and your opponents second-guessing. When you present yourself with open, strong body language, your brain takes note and reinforces that self-assurance. What's really cool is that when your team sees you stand tall and confident, it lifts their spirits, too. It builds an unspoken trust and boosts everybody's energy level.

Posture and Presence

Now, let's chat about proper posture. Standing tall isn't just about looking cool; it actually helps you breathe better. You won't be bent over gasping for air. And that upright stance? It helps you speak and shout out plays or encouragement more clearly. This leads to stronger performances because you're not just talking the talk but walking the walk—literally! Having a good posture allows you to fill your lungs completely, which means more oxygen to fuel your muscles and brain (Murphy, 2024). Another tip: Coaches are also looking at your posture and body language, so consider what they may be thinking when they see your great posture. So, next time you're out there, keep those shoulders back and chin up. Think of it as putting on your superhero cape!

What About Facial Expressions?

Next up is smiling. Yes, smiling! Even in the middle of an intense game, flashing a quick smile can work wonders. A smile tells your brain everything's all right, making you feel happier and less stressed even if you're playing against tough competition. Smiling creates this awesome loop where your mood lifts, you play better, and then you smile even more—it's infectious! Research has shown that smiling can elevate your mood and ultimately improve performance in sports (Taylor, 2023).

Practical Techniques

But let's get practical here. How exactly do you build this habit of confidence in your body language? Well, practicing specific poses can make it natural for you to feel more confident. Before a game, try adopting what some call "power poses." These are broad stances where you take up space, just like victory poses with your hands on hips or arms raised triumphantly. Spend a couple of minutes standing like this in the locker room, and let it psych you up for the challenge ahead.

Another simple yet powerful technique is using affirmations. Have you ever tried telling yourself, "I've got this" or "I'm ready" just before stepping onto the field? It sounds cheesy, but speaking positive words out loud or in your mind can hype you up. It preps your brain to perform at its best by reinforcing that you believe in your abilities.

Exercise: Body Language Confidence Boost for Softball Athletes

Objective: To help you improve your body language and boost self-esteem through practical techniques.

Instructions:

- **Confidence poses practice**

    o   Find a calm space where you can stand tall without distractions.

    o   Stand in front of a mirror or imagine how you want to appear to others.

    o   Practice three "confidence poses" for two minutes each:

        ▪   **Supergirl pose:** Stand tall with your feet shoulder-width apart, hands on your hips, and chest out.

        ▪   **Victory pose:** Raise your arms above your head in a 'V' shape, smiling and holding the pose for a minute.

        ▪   **Power pose:** Stand with one foot slightly in front of the other, arms crossed over your chest, and take deep breaths. Hold this pose for two minutes.

- **Positive affirmations**

    o   Write down three positive affirmations that resonate with you, such as:

        ▪   "I am strong and capable."

        ▪   "I trust my skills and my training."

        ▪   "I am a confident and valuable team member."

    o   Repeat these affirmations aloud while standing in your confidence pose.

    o   Write your own in the space provided:

1. _____

2. _____

3. _____

- **Mindful body language adjustments**

32

- Choose a comfortable spot and close your eyes for a moment.

- Take deep breaths and focus on your body. Notice how it feels in different postures (slouching vs. standing tall).

- Sit up straight and place your hands on your thighs, feet flat on the ground. While sitting, practice:

  - Relaxing your shoulders.

  - Keeping your chin up and looking straight ahead.

- Remind yourself of your positive affirmations during this exercise.

- **Body language awareness in practice**

  - During warm-ups or practice, pay attention to your body language and that of your teammates.

  - Take note of moments when you feel confident and compare them to moments when you feel less confident.

  - Make mental notes of physical changes, such as posture or facial expressions, during different activities.

- **Team support and sharing**

  - After practice, gather your teammates and share your favorite confidence poses and affirmations.

  - Encourage each other to practice these techniques regularly, creating a supportive environment where everyone builds confidence together.

By practicing these techniques, you'll improve your body language and boost your self-esteem. How you carry yourself can impact your performance and the energy you bring to your team!

Bringing It Home

In this chapter, we've explored how building confidence can greatly impact your sports performance and personal growth. Confidence isn't something you can just wish into existence; it's developed through self-awareness, understanding your unique strengths, and consistent practice. Remember, the more time you spend improving your skills in softball, the stronger that inner belief becomes. Trusting in your training helps during those crucial game moments, making decision-making smoother and actions more effective. Your focus improves with higher confidence levels, allowing you to block out doubts and perform at your best. And yes, even when things don't go as planned, confidence builds resilience, helping you bounce back and learn from setbacks.

As a young athlete, recognizing your strengths is the key to boosting your confidence in and out of the game. Identifying what you're good at not only inspires you but also sets a clear path toward achieving realistic goals. Emphasizing your strengths empowers you to excel in your role and builds a positive self-image. This positive outlook encourages a mindset shift, approaching challenges with determination rather than doubt. Stand tall with confident body language, breathe deeply, and maybe throw in a smile—these small changes can make a big difference. As you continue your journey in sports, know that every bit of confidence you build now lays the foundation for becoming an unstoppable player and individual.

Chapter 4: Resilience—Bouncing Back from Setbacks

You can't always control the circumstances, only how you react to those circumstances; you can always control your attitude and your effort. – Jennie Finch

Bouncing back from setbacks is an essential skill in sports, especially in softball. It's the ability to recover quickly from difficulties that sets apart great athletes from good ones. Resilience is not just about being tough; it's about managing obstacles and coming out stronger every time. Imagine walking up to the plate after striking out in your last game or stepping back on the field after making a mistake—that's resilience in action. It's important for athletes to harness this inner strength to keep pushing forward despite setbacks. This chapter will explore how you can accept mistakes, learn from them, and build the mental toughness needed to thrive in competitive sports.

We'll dive into real strategies that will help you develop your resilience as an athlete. When you shift your mindset, you can see mistakes as valuable learning opportunities rather than failures. We'll uncover techniques such as adopting a growth-oriented mindset, setting achievable goals, and building a supportive environment that encourages self-improvement. Plus, highlighting real-life examples of athletes who have faced challenges head-on and emerged winners showcases that true success lies not just in winning games but also in developing the persistence and positive attitude to stand up after falling down. This path to resilience equips you with the tools you need not only in sports but also in life as you learn to move through challenges with confidence and determination.

What It Means to Be Resilient in Softball

Resilience is not just about being strong; it's about how you handle adversity and rise above it. In the world of competitive sports, you often deal with changes in performance, injuries, and the pressure of expectations. Resilience helps you stay focused and determined even when things don't go as planned.

Understanding that challenges are stepping stones rather than roadblocks can change everything. Mistakes on the field aren't failures; they're opportunities to grow and learn. It's vital to adopt an attitude where mistakes are seen as part of the journey to improvement. When you mess up during a game, instead of hanging your head, think about what it teaches you. Maybe it's that you need to practice your swing more or communicate better with teammates. Each challenge teaches something new, making you a stronger, smarter athlete.

The Role of Mindset

A big part of building resilience is having a positive and adaptive mindset.

So, what exactly is a positive mindset? A positive mindset means thinking in a way that helps you see the good side of things, even when challenges come up. It's about staying optimistic, believing in your ability to improve, and focusing on what you can do rather than getting stuck on what's going wrong.

This means looking at setbacks not as defeats but as lessons. This shift in perspective changes everything. Instead of thinking, "I failed," consider asking, "What is this experience trying to teach me?" It's about turning negative experiences into learning moments. An adaptive mindset empowers you to recover mentally, changing failures into a springboard for future success. Coaches and mentors are key in helping you develop this mindset by encouraging you to focus on growth and improvement rather than dwelling on mistakes.

Specifically, in softball, this could mean working tirelessly on batting techniques if that's where you struggle most. The growth-oriented mindset strengthens the idea that talent isn't fixed; it's something you build over time.

A useful guideline to nurture this mindset is to set specific, achievable goals. Having clear ideas provides direction and purpose, like improving pitching accuracy or boosting teamwork skills. By breaking down larger ambitions into smaller, manageable tasks, you can track progress and celebrate wins along the way. This not only strengthens confidence but also reinforces the belief in your ability to improve continuously.

Real-Life Examples

Consider real-life examples of resilient young athletes who have faced challenges head-on.

Bethany Hamilton: A Shark Attack Couldn't Stop Her

Imagine being 13 years old and already one of the best young surfers in the world. That was Bethany Hamilton in 2003. But then, while surfing off the coast of Hawaii, a 14-foot tiger shark attacked her, taking her left arm (*10 Inspiring Examples of Highly Resilient Sportspeople*, n.d.).

For most people, this would have been the end of their surfing dreams. But not for Bethany. Just one month after the attack, she was back in the water, learning to surf with one arm. By the next year, she was competing again—and winning.

Bethany's story is a powerful reminder that setbacks can't hold you back if your mindset is strong. She chose to focus on what she could do, not what she had lost. Today, she's not only a professional surfer but also an author and motivational speaker, inspiring athletes everywhere to stay determined.

Abby Wambach: From Injury to World Champion

Abby Wambach was 25 and at the top of her game as a star player for the U.S. Women's National Soccer Team when disaster struck. Just before the 2008 Olympics, she suffered a devastating broken leg. The injury not only crushed her Olympic dreams but also put her entire career in jeopardy (*10 Inspiring Examples of Highly Resilient Sportspeople*, n.d.).

But Abby didn't let that stop her. She threw herself into rehab, working harder than ever to regain her strength. By 2015, Abby was back—and better than ever. She led the U.S. team to a historic victory in the FIFA Women's World Cup.

Her story shows that resilience isn't just about bouncing back—it's about using challenges as fuel to become stronger. Abby's mindset of never giving up turned a career-threatening injury into a defining moment of her success.

Practice Letting Go of Mistakes Immediately and Refocusing

When playing sports, it's important to quickly move past mistakes and focus on the next play. Let's look at some great strategies to make this happen.

Instant Recovery Techniques

First up are instant recovery techniques, which are excellent for resetting your mind after a mistake.

- **Deep breathing:** Whenever you feel stressed or frustrated about a play that didn't go your way, take a slow, deep breath. Inhale through your nose, filling your lungs completely, then exhale slowly through your mouth. This action can calm your nerves and bring your focus back to the present moment.

- **Positive self-talk:** Say things to yourself like "I can do this" or "Next time will be better" to shift your mindset from negative to positive. This simple adjustment can lift your spirits and prepare you mentally for what comes next.

- **Relying on your teammates:** Lean into your teammates to help you reset. If they give you a "high-five," that is your reset. They believe that you can make the next play and that high-five resets your mind to believe it, too.

Exercise: Instant Recovery Techniques for Softball Athletes

The goal of this exercise is to help you develop instant recovery techniques to overcome mistakes and maintain a positive mindset during games.

Instructions:

- **Deep breathing practice**

    - Find a quiet spot where you can focus without interruptions.

    - Sit or stand comfortably. Close your eyes if it helps you concentrate.

    - Take a deep breath in through your nose for a count of four, filling your lungs completely.

    - Hold your breath for a count of four.

    - Exhale slowly through your mouth for a count of six, releasing all the air.

    - Repeat this cycle five times, focusing on calming your mind and body.

- **Positive self-talk**

    - After your breathing practice, write down a recent mistake you made in a game or during practice.

_____
_____
_____
_____
_____

    - Now, write down three positive self-talk phrases that you can use next time you face a similar situation, such as:

        - "I learn from my mistakes and grow stronger."

        - "I have the skills to bounce back."

- ■ "I will focus on my next opportunity."

1. _____

2. _____

3. _____

- ○ Repeat these phrases out loud, imagining yourself in a game situation where you can apply them.

- **Quick recovery techniques**

  - ○ During your next practice or training session, pay attention to your reactions after making a mistake (e.g., missing a catch or making an error).

  - ○ When you make a mistake, immediately use one of your positive self-talk phrases and follow it with a deep breath.

  - ○ Allow yourself a moment to acknowledge the mistake, then visualize letting it go as you exhale.

- **Mental habit building**

  - ○ Set up a game-like scenario during practice with your teammates (e.g., scrimmage or drills).

  - ○ Instruct everyone to practice instant recovery techniques after any mistakes.

  - ○ Encourage them to use deep breathing and positive self-talk aloud when mistakes happen.

  - ○ Celebrate quick recoveries, reinforcing the idea that bouncing back is part of being a great athlete.

- **Reflection and sharing**

  - ○ After your practice, gather your teammates and discuss how instant recovery techniques worked for everyone.

  - ○ Share experiences where you successfully used these methods and how it felt.

  - ○ Encourage each other to keep practicing these techniques in upcoming games and training sessions.

Practicing instant recovery techniques helps athletes reset their minds and let go of mistakes. The more you use these methods, the more instinctive they will become, allowing you to perform confidently in high-stakes situations!

The Next Play Mentality

Another helpful concept is adopting a "next play" mentality. Sports are fast-paced, and dwelling on mistakes can cause you to miss out on future opportunities. When you focus on the next play, you keep your momentum going without getting bogged down by mistakes made. Think of it as turning a page in a book; you can't get wrapped up in one chapter if you want to enjoy the rest of the story. Athletes who consistently look forward after setbacks tend to maintain their energy levels and stay in the zone.

Building mental habits is key. Remember, these strategies aren't just one-time tricks. They require practice and consistency. Regularly integrating deep breathing into your routine will help it become second nature when you're feeling stressed. Consciously remind yourself to focus on the next play each time you step onto the field. The more you practice these techniques, the more natural they'll become, boosting your overall performance and resilience over time.

Staying Focused Under Pressure

Keeping your concentration under pressure is important if you want to excel. When the stakes are high and the adrenaline is pumping, having a strategy to stay focused can boost your performance. Understanding that pressure is a normal part of sports is key to developing great coping strategies. Recognizing that everyone experiences it helps normalize the sensation and reduces the stigma or fear associated with it. You can then see pressure as a friend rather than an enemy.

The Importance of Mindfulness Techniques

Mindfulness exercises are an excellent way to center focus and ground you when you feel overwhelmed. Techniques such as deep breathing or body scanning help shift attention back to the present moment, where it belongs during competition. For example, taking a few seconds to inhale deeply through the nose and slowly exhale can calm nerves and refocus the mind on what needs to be done next (Crim, 2023a). These moments of mindfulness encourage you to engage fully in what they're doing now rather than worrying about past mistakes or future outcomes.

Pregame Routines

Pre-game routines are important in reducing anxiety and signaling readiness for action. Establishing a familiar routine creates a sense of control and comfort. Whether it's listening to a specific playlist, performing certain stretches, or visualizing success, these rituals prepare the mind and body for peak performance. When you follow a set routine, it's like telling your brain, "I'm ready for this," which helps diminish pre-game jitters and boosts confidence.

Rituals allow you to enter a focused mindset, signaling to your brain that it's time for action. For example, if you're on defense, know where the play is going before the ball is hit to you. If you're batting, time the pitcher in the on-deck circle. These are routines that help set the players up for success during the game.

Staying Composed During Competition

During high-pressure situations, maintaining composure by breaking tasks into small, manageable steps prevents overwhelm. Instead of focusing on the huge event in front of you or its possible outcomes, concentrating on one play or move at a time keeps things simple and achievable. For instance, a softball player might focus only on their grip and stance before swinging instead of worrying about the final score. This targeted approach helps you stay calm and collected, making it easier to perform under pressure (Dailyhuman, 2024).

Staying focused under pressure requires intention and practice. The next play mentality encourages you to quickly move on from a mistake to maintain their momentum. Instead of dwelling on an error, the focus shifts to what comes next, using positive self-talk or imagery to reset the mind. This forward focus helps in keeping spirits high and encourages resilience during competitions.

Reflective practice is an important exercise for strengthening future performance. After the game, reviewing what went well and where improvements can be made promotes constructive analysis. This reflection turns mistakes into learning opportunities, thereby boosting mental toughness and preparing you better for subsequent challenges.

Bringing It Home

In this chapter, we've focused on how accepting mistakes can build resilience and mental toughness in softball. We've learned that errors are not the end but opportunities to grow stronger. Viewing challenges as a path forward rather than roadblocks is key to developing a resilient mindset. We discussed techniques like deep breathing, positive self-talk, and visualization—practical tools every athlete can use to bounce back from setbacks quickly.

As we wrap up, remember that building mental toughness takes practice and patience. Focusing on growth and keeping a positive attitude allows you to pave the way for success—not just in softball but in whatever challenges you tackle next.

In the next chapter, we'll jump into focus. Why is it so important?

Chapter 5: Focus—Staying Present in the Game

Try not to get lost in comparing yourself to others. Discover your gifts and let them shine! – Jennie Finch

Staying present in the game is all about sharpening your focus. In competitive sports like softball, keeping your attention on the task at hand can really boost your performance. But it's not just about blocking out distractions; it's about zeroing in on what truly matters during play. This chapter explores how an unwavering focus can be your secret weapon on the field. When you're dialed in, every pitch feels more manageable, and each catch becomes an opportunity to showcase your best self. Focus helps strengthen decision-making, guiding you through intense moments with clarity and precision. When you develop a strong mental game, you can shift from just playing to being really successful under pressure.

With that said, how exactly do you train your brain to stay focused during the heat of competition? This chapter dives into strategies to sharpen your mental skills. You'll learn simple yet powerful methods to help boost your concentration and handle tough situations easily. We'll cover practical routines you can use in your daily practice to improve your focus steadily over time. Whether it's mental cues to bring your mind back when it starts to drift or creating focus rituals before games, these tools are designed to help keep you steady and sharp. The path to mastery begins with understanding and applying these insights, turning potential distractions into opportunities for growth.

How Focus Helps You Perform Better

In the world of sports, focus is key. Being present in the moment can make all the difference in your performance. Let's look into how maintaining focus can elevate your gameplay and why so many athletes prioritize it as a critical component of their success.

Understanding Concentration

First off, having focused concentration improves your decision-making skills and execution during sports. Imagine you're on the field; every play demands quick thinking and precise actions. When you're fully focused, your brain processes information more effectively, allowing you to make better decisions, whether it's deciding when to swing the bat or which base to throw to (Cherry, 2023). This enhanced decision-making ability leads to more accurate plays and a higher chance of achieving your goals during a game.

The Impact of Distractions

It's super common to get distracted by things around you when you're out on the field. Maybe you hear your parents yelling from the stands, or the other team is cheering loudly. Sometimes, it feels like the umpire isn't making the right calls, and that can be super frustrating. But guess what? Those things are totally out of your control. The best thing you can do is learn to focus on what you can control—like your attitude, your effort, and how you play the game.

Recognizing those distractions is the first step in stopping them from affecting your performance. You might think, "Wow, that loud cheer is really bothering me," but when you pinpoint it, it becomes easier to brush it off and stay in the game.

Understanding the physics of the game helps, too! When you're at bat or pitching, thinking about how to use your body, your grip, and your timing can keep your mind locked on the task instead of worrying about the noise around you.

And hey, even the pros get distracted! Take a look at some high-profile games where distractions had a real impact. There've been moments where big calls have made players lose their focus, affecting the final scores.

If you speak to successful athletes about their secret to performing at high levels consistently, many will mention focus as a core component. They often attribute their ability to stay dialed in during important moments to meticulous mental preparation and a conscious effort to drown out distractions.

So, how can you incorporate these strategies into your routine? Here are some practical guidelines:

- **Start with pre-performance routines:** Develop a pre-game ritual that gets you in the zone. It could be something like visualizing the upcoming plays or simply spending a few quiet moments focusing on your breathing. Routines like this help establish a positive mindset and sharpen concentration.

- **Daily visualization practice:** Just like physical training, consistency is key. Dedicate time each day to visualize different aspects of your game. Picture yourself successfully executing skills and strategies. Consider all senses. Imagine the sound of the ball against your bat or the feel of running bases. Over time, your ability to focus will improve, making you more prepared for real-world scenarios (Crim, 2023a).

- **Create specific focus cues:** Identify cues that help bring your attention back when it starts to wander. It might be a keyword like "focus" or a deep breath. Having these cues readily available during games can quickly re-center your mind, keeping you aligned with your objectives. Write down what your mental cues are going to be.

_____

_____

_____

_____

_____

_____

_____

By integrating these techniques, you'll find yourself more capable of handling the pressures of competition while also enjoying the game more deeply. Remember, focus isn't just about shutting out distractions; it's about accepting the moment and channeling your energy toward your goals.

With patience and perseverance, staying focused becomes an integral part of how you approach sports. Training your mind is just as important as training your body because the two work together to unlock your full potential on the field. Keep practicing these techniques, and watch how your focus changes your athletic performance, making you a stronger, more resilient competitor ready for anything thrown your way.

Avoiding Distractions

Staying focused during a game can be challenging. Distractions are everywhere, but learning how to manage them means everything. Let's look at how to minimize distractions both during a game and beyond.

Identifying Personal Distractions

First, identifying personal distractions is a necessary step in managing them well. One thing common to all female athletes, yet seldom talked about is how menstruation can affect training and play. For many, dealing with menstrual pain poses an interruption and distraction. Knowing your cycle allows for proactive management, such as taking pain-relief medications before symptoms start or adjusting training intensity around those times. This foresight reduces the distraction potential, allowing you to keep your head in the game. Don't hesitate to reach out to your coach or teammates for suggestions or advice.

You could also be distracted by equipment that doesn't fit right. Frequently, in female sports, you end up with items designed for men that don't fit comfortably. Or maybe you're trying to get an extra season out of last year's cleats despite that pinching feeling in your toe?

Whatever they are, identifying what your personal distractions are is where to begin.

Strategies for Managing Distractions

Strategies aimed at handling distractions can also involve mental cues and breathing techniques. These are practical tips you can use the moment you realize you're losing focus. Think of mental cues as your brain's yellow sticky notes—they serve as reminders to bring yourself back to the present moment. A simple phrase like "eye on the ball" or even a visual cue can work wonders. Pairing this with deep breathing exercises helps calm your mind and body. Breathing techniques, like inhaling slowly through the nose and exhaling longer than the inhale, can reset your focus. These practices help you feel centered, especially in high-pressure moments during gameplay, where maintaining concentration is vital.

Exercise: Strategies for Managing Distractions for Softball Athletes

The goal of this exercise is to help you develop practical strategies to filter out distractions, refocus, and improve concentration during games and practices.

Instructions:

- **Identifying distractions**

    - Take a moment to think about distractions you might encounter during games or practices (e.g., loud crowds, sideline chatter, menstrual pain, or your own thoughts).

    - Write down at least three distractions that commonly affect your focus.

1. _____

2. _____

3. _____

- Next, write each distraction and note how it makes you feel and how it impacts your performance.

_____

_____

_____

_____

_____

_____

_____

_____

_____

_____

_____

- **Creating mental cues**

  - Think of a simple word or phrase that will serve as your mental cue to refocus (e.g., "Focus," "Breathe," or "Eyes on the ball").

  - Practice saying this word or phrase quietly to yourself while visualizing it as a sign to redirect your thoughts.

  - During practice, use your cue when you feel distracted to reinforce its effect. Write down your mental cue.

_____

_____

_____

_____

_____

_____

_____

- **Developing a pre-play routine**

  - Create a personal pre-play routine you can follow before every pitch, swing, or play. This can be a sequence of actions or phrases that help you focus.

  - Your routine might include:

    - Taking two deep breaths.

    - Saying your mental cue out loud.

    - Visualizing the play you want to execute.

- ■ Moving your feet to shift your stance or setting your glove in place.

  - ○ Practice this routine during practice sessions so that it becomes second nature.

- **Putting it all together**

  - ○ During your next scrimmage or practice, consciously use your mental cues, breathing techniques, and pre-play routine to manage distractions.

  - ○ In the space below, reflect on how all these strategies worked for you and share your experiences with a teammate or coach.

_____
_____
_____
_____
_____
_____
_____
_____
_____
_____
_____
_____
_____
_____

Managing distractions is essential for peak performance in softball. By implementing these strategies and practices, you'll improve your focus and concentration, allowing you to perform your best in high-pressure situations!

The Scoop on Team Distractions

Understanding team dynamics is important in making sure peer interactions don't become a source of distraction. On a team, everyone has different personalities and ways of communicating, which can sometimes clash or create tension. To maintain concentration, it's beneficial to understand each teammate's communication style and try to build a supportive environment rather than one filled with conflict. Having regular open conversations about how each person likes to receive feedback or handle mistakes makes it easier to prevent misunderstandings from becoming distractions during the game. Establishing clear roles and responsibilities within the team can also help members stay focused on their tasks without being sidetracked by what's happening around them.

Environmental Considerations

Environmental factors are another potential distraction that require adaptation to maintain focus. Weather conditions, like extreme heat, cold, or rain, can all affect performance and concentration levels. Before a game, it's helpful to check the forecast and prepare accordingly. Dressing in layers, staying hydrated, or having towels to wipe away rain or sweat can lessen the impact of these environmental distractions. Additionally, becoming physically and mentally resilient to unexpected weather changes builds your ability to adapt quickly and keep your focus on the game. Practicing under different weather conditions can also make you comfortable with performing regardless of environmental challenges.

Setting Specific, Measurable Goals for Each Practice and Game

Goal-setting is a powerful tool in sports. It helps you to zero in on what matters most and keeps your mind sharp during intense games. When you set clear goals, you create a roadmap that not only guides your actions but also lets you track how far you've come throughout the season. When you know exactly what you want to achieve, every practice becomes an opportunity to work toward that target. This focus is critical in maintaining enthusiasm and motivation, especially when facing challenges.

SMART Goals Framework

To make sure your goals are as effective as possible, it's essential to use the SMART criteria. This acronym stands for specific, measurable, achievable, relevant, and time-bound. Let's break it down (Stibich, 2024):

- **Specific:** Your goals need to be specific, meaning they should be clear and detailed so you know exactly what you're aiming for. If you're a softball player, instead of saying, "I want to improve my batting," you could set a goal like "I want to increase my batting average by 0.10 by the end of the season." This way, you have a precise target.

- **Measurable:** Next, goals should be measurable. You need to have a way to track your progress and see if you're moving closer to your goal. Using numbers or benchmarks can help with this. For instance, if your goal is to run faster, timing your runs in each practice session will allow you to see improvements over time.

- **Achievable:** When we talk about achievable goals, it's crucial that your goals are realistic, given your abilities and resources. Setting a goal that's too far out of reach can be discouraging, while a goal that's too easy might not push you enough. Aim for that sweet spot where your goal challenges you but isn't impossible.

- **Relevant:** Goals should also be relevant to what you want to achieve in your sports journey. They should align with your long-term aspirations and be meaningful to you personally, whether it's mastering a particular skill or improving teamwork.

- **Time-bound:** Finally, time-bound means setting a deadline for your goals. This adds urgency and keeps you accountable. Whether it's a week, a month, or a full season, having a timeframe helps you organize your efforts and manage your time effectively.

Creating Accountability

Beyond just setting goals, creating a system of accountability can be really helpful. Sharing your goals with teammates is a great start. When others know what you're working toward, it builds a supportive environment where everyone encourages each other. This team spirit not only strengthens individual performance but boosts the entire team's morale. Check-ins with friends or coaches about your progress can keep you motivated and committed.

Reflective Practices

Reflective practices are key in reinforcing your focus and assessing your performance. After each game, take some time to jot down your thoughts in a journal. Write about:

- What went well?

- What didn't go as planned?

- What did you learn from the experience?

Reflecting on both wins and setbacks helps you recognize patterns in your performance and identify areas for improvement. This kind of self-assessment not only solidifies what you've learned but also boosts your focus on future games.

By integrating these practices into your sports routine, you develop a stronger mental game. These strategies equip you with the skills to not only excel in softball but also carry valuable lessons into other competitive sports and life itself.

Bringing It Home

In this chapter, we've explored how focus and goal-setting are powerful tools for strengthening athletic performance. By staying present and concentrating on the task at hand, you can make better decisions and respond more effectively during games. These methods not only sharpen skills but also boost confidence, making every game an opportunity to shine.

Now it's your turn to put these strategies into action. Remember, mastering focus and goal-setting doesn't happen overnight. Start integrating visualization and focus cues into your routine, and watch as your gameplay changes. Keep your goals clear and track your progress along the way. Don't be afraid to tweak them as necessary, so they're challenging yet achievable. Reflect often on your experiences, both successes and setbacks, to understand what works best for you. With patience and persistence, you'll find yourself growing not just as an athlete but as someone who is resilient and determined in every aspect of life.

It's time to move into the next chapter, where we'll discuss what it means to be a part of a team.

Chapter 6: Teamwork—Supporting Your Teammates

The team with the best athletes doesn't usually win. It's the team with the athletes who play best together. –Lisa Fernandez

Supporting your teammates isn't just about being friendly; it's about strengthening the entire team. When you're in the middle of a tough softball game, nothing is better than knowing your teammates have your back. This solid bond makes everyone perform better and more confidently, whether you're making that perfect catch or cheering from the sidelines. Being supportive doesn't just strengthen your confidence; it builds a team where everyone feels valued and motivated to give their best. When you're aware of each person's unique strengths and contributions, you create an environment where positivity grows and performance soars.

This chapter looks at how building team chemistry through support, communication, and leadership can uplift you and your team in amazing ways. You'll learn techniques for recognizing and celebrating each other's achievements, big or small. We will explore how constructive feedback can be shared without discouraging one another and why open communication is the bedrock of trust within your team. You'll discover strategies for building a supportive atmosphere in the game and in life, making those bonds even stronger.

How to Be a Supportive Teammate

Being a pillar of support for your teammates is necessary for building a positive and cohesive team environment. When everyone feels valued for what they can contribute, it leads to an atmosphere filled with respect and appreciation. Think about it like this: Each player on your team brings something special to the table. Maybe one player is amazing at strategizing, while another excels in keeping up team morale during tough times. Recognizing these individual strengths doesn't only make each person feel good, but it also elevates the whole team's performance.

For instance, let's consider a situation where a teammate hits a home run or makes a crucial catch during a softball game. Acknowledging their effort and impact can reinforce positive behaviors and motivate them to continue putting in their best effort. This appreciation extends beyond major accomplishments, too—even recognizing someone for supporting a fellow player during practice, like offering water or words of encouragement, builds mutual respect among teammates.

Offering Constructive Feedback

Now, let's talk about feedback. There's a fine line between constructive feedback and plain criticism. The key lies in being specific and focusing on improvement. Instead of saying, "You played terribly," opt for feedback like, "I've struggled with that, too. What helped me was adjusting my stance to improve accuracy. Maybe you could give that a try?" This approach not only points out areas for growth but also offers advice that encourages improvement. Being specific with your feedback helps teammates understand what they need to work on without feeling attacked or discouraged.

One example of effective feedback might be during a pitching session. If a pitcher consistently throws too high, rather than critiquing their ability broadly, as a teammate, you could suggest, "Aim slightly lower next time; it could help you hit the strike zone more effectively." This kind of guidance respects the player's existing skills while still promoting growth.

Creating a Safe Space for Sharing

Open communication is another great way to create a supportive team environment. When you make sure there's space for everyone to share thoughts and feelings openly, you build trust. When your fellow teammates know they can speak up or confide in you without fear of judgment, they're more likely to contribute valuable ideas. For instance, if a strategy isn't working during a game, teammates who communicate well can quickly adjust tactics by considering everyone's input. These environments encourage honesty, where everyone feels comfortable discussing what works and what doesn't.

It also helps to have regular team meetings where everyone has the chance to voice opinions and suggestions, which can start this openness. These discussions are often when quieter voices get heard, bringing fresh perspectives to the table. Building open communication isn't just about talking; it also involves active listening. Paying attention when your teammates speak shows that you value their input, further strengthening trust within your team.

Celebrating Teammates' Success

Don't underestimate the power of celebrating successes together. Whether it's after a big win or a personal achievement from a team member, taking the time to acknowledge these moments boosts morale in a huge way. Celebrations don't always have to be massive—sometimes, simple acts like giving shout-outs during practice or sending congratulatory messages in group chats are enough to show appreciation.

Let's say your team wins a local tournament or a single intense match. Organizing a small post-game celebration can cement bonds and give everyone a sense of shared accomplishment. These celebrations are about more than just winning; they emphasize the hard work everyone puts into reaching that point, reinforcing the idea that each contribution is important.

By promoting an environment where each person plays a part in recognizing and uplifting each other, you create a culture of positivity. This not only strengthens current relationships but also lays a strong foundation for lasting connections in the future. When teammates support each other through highs and lows, it builds resilience. This collective strength becomes invaluable, especially during challenging periods throughout the sports season or even beyond the field in life.

Building Trust and Communication On and Off the Field

Trust and open communication are the foundations of any successful team, especially for young athletes striving to improve their performance in sports like softball. Imagine your team is a well-oiled machine. Trust is like the oil that keeps all the parts moving smoothly, and open communication is the grease that guarantees nothing grinds to a halt.

Team Building Activities

Team-building activities are a great way to build trust and open lines of communication by bringing your teammates together in settings that are often more relaxed than practice or game situations. For instance, a weekend hike or even a simple group picnic can break the ice, allowing teammates to learn about each other beyond the field.

This personal connection translates into better collaboration during games. When you know your teammate's preferences, strengths, and quirks, communicating on the field becomes second nature. According to Dr. Robert Gordon, encouraging feedback and creating opportunities for honest exchanges can also boost team dynamics (Gordon, 2023).

For team-building activities, consider events that cater to different interests within the team. Not everyone will enjoy the same type of activity, so having a range of options can make sure the whole team feels included. Maybe a game of mini-golf, a cooking class, or an escape room challenge? The goal is to create an environment where your teammates can bond over something fun and unrelated to their sport. Team-building doesn't have to be formal or expensive; even short bonding sessions during practice breaks can make an impact.

Establishing Effective Communication

Understanding different communication styles is just as important for preventing misunderstandings within the team. You might notice that some teammates are direct and get straight to the point, while others may prefer a more roundabout way of expressing themselves. Recognizing these differences can help you understand messages correctly and avoid potential conflicts. It's like learning a new language; once you master it, everything flows more freely. When roles and expectations are communicated clearly, team members are more likely to engage actively and collaborate effectively.

When establishing communication that works within teammates, regular check-ins can keep everyone on the same page. Weekly team meetings or biweekly one-on-ones with coaches can offer a space for expressing thoughts and ideas without the pressure of immediate responses.

Talk to your coach about an "open door" policy, where team members feel comfortable discussing concerns privately if needed. Having a culture of openness requires effort from everyone, so leading by example is important. Show your teammates that it's okay to be honest by being transparent about your own thoughts and feelings.

Practicing Active Listening

Active listening isn't just about hearing words; it's about understanding the intent behind those words and responding thoughtfully. Imagine a scenario where a teammate brings up a concern about a play. Instead of immediately offering solutions, take a moment to reflect on what they are really saying. Are they worried about how the play affects their position, or are they concerned about the overall team strategy? When you actively listen, you not only resolve conflicts but also strengthen teamwork.

To practice active listening, adopt techniques like:

- Repeat back what the speaker said.

- Ask clarifying questions.

- Refrain from interrupting.

Simple gestures such as nodding or maintaining eye contact can show that you're fully engaged in the conversation. Incorporating role-playing exercises during practice can help develop these skills in real-time scenarios. Remember, active listening isn't just about resolving issues—it's about making every teammate feel valued and heard.

Creating Teams Goals Together

Involving all players in goal-setting sessions can be a game-changer. When everyone has a say in setting team goals, it creates a sense of ownership and commitment. Think of it as planting seeds together; everyone waters them, guaranteeing that the goals bloom into achievements. When team members agree on objectives collectively, there's a stronger drive to achieve them because it feels like a shared mission rather than something imposed by the coach or captains. Studies show that role clarity and involvement can lead to increased satisfaction and cooperation within the team (Gail, 2023).

When aiming to establish team goals, try to include everyone in brainstorming sessions. Maybe the team could make individual vision boards where players jot down personal aspirations, which can then be integrated into the team's broader objectives. This approach makes sure that personal development lines up with team growth. Celebrate small wins along the way to keep motivation levels high on your team. Acknowledging progress, no matter how minor, reinforces that everyone's input is driving the team forward.

How to Be a Role Model in Practice and Games

In the world of sports, how you carry yourself can really influence your team. Demonstrating sportsmanship and resilience is about more than just winning or losing—it's about setting an example that inspires those around you. Let's say you're in the middle of a softball game where tensions are high, and the score is close. In these moments, a player who shows respect for opponents, follows the rules, and keeps cool under pressure sets a powerful standard for their teammates. This attitude builds an environment of fair play and integrity, which naturally uplifts team spirit and camaraderie. Sportsmanship is not just about the game; it's a lifestyle choice that echoes in every part of life. A positive attitude builds a culture where everyone feels included and valued, aligning with what it means to be a true team player.

Being Dependable

Being dependable is another key aspect that grounds a strong team dynamic. When teammates know they can count on each other, magic happens. Reliability involves showing up to practice, giving 100% effort in games, and staying committed, rain or shine. This consistency builds mutual trust among team members. It's like when someone sees you sprinting to practice after school—they notice your dedication, and it encourages them to match it. By being reliable, you create a foundation of trust and accountability within the team. An easy way to build this kind of reliability is by keeping open lines of communication with your coach and teammates, making sure everyone is aware of commitments and expectations.

Encouraging a Growth Mindset

Encouraging a growth mindset is important for any athlete striving for personal and team success. This means believing talents and abilities can be developed through hard work and feedback. Encouraging your fellow teammates to adopt this mindset helps them look at challenges as opportunities rather than obstacles. Picture a teammate struggling with her batting technique—rather than getting discouraged, she works on it every day, uses tips from her coach, and gradually sees improvement. Her perseverance teaches everyone that it's okay to make mistakes as long as you're willing to learn from them. A growth mindset doesn't just improve individual performance; it creates a supportive environment where taking risks and learning from them becomes the norm.

Maintaining a Positive Attitude

When you maintain optimism, especially during challenging times, it changes the energy of the entire team. It's normal for games to have ups and downs, and how you handle those moments says a lot about your character. Staying positive when faced with setbacks helps keep morale high and boost confidence levels among your peers. If you're playing and the other team scores a home run, instead of letting it get you down, focus on the next play and encourage your team with words like, "We got this!" Positivity is infectious, providing the lift needed to rally and refocus your efforts. Optimistic players remind everyone that every challenge is an opportunity to grow stronger together.

To strengthen these behaviors, you could implement a few practical guidelines. For instance, being dependable might involve using a shared calendar app to track practice schedules and ensure punctuality. Encouraging a growth mindset can be supported by setting small, achievable goals each week—perhaps mastering a new skill or strengthening an existing one—and celebrating progress along the way. These simple steps not only boost personal development but also contribute to a strong and resilient team culture.

Pre-Game Preparation Exercise: Personalizing Your Routine

Objective: To enhance your mindset and prepare for your upcoming softball game by reflecting on and personalizing your pre-game routine.

Instructions:

- **Find a quiet space:** Settle into a comfortable and quiet space where you can think and write without distractions.

- **Reflect on the night before the game:**

  o Write down what you had for dinner. Was it nutritious and energizing?

  _____
  _____
  _____
  _____
  _____

  o Did you drink enough water? How much did you hydrate yourself?

  _____
  _____
  _____
  _____
  _____

  o What time did you go to sleep? Was it enough rest to feel energized for the game?

  _____
  _____
  _____
  _____
  _____

- **List your evening activities:**

  - Note any other activities you engaged in the night before. Did you review your game plan, visualize your performance, or do any stretching?

  _____

  _____

  _____

  _____

  _____

  - Reflect on how these activities contributed to your readiness.

  _____

  _____

  _____

  _____

  _____

- **Next morning checklist:**

  - Write down what you did the next morning after waking up. Did you eat a healthy breakfast? What did you choose to fuel your body?

  _____

  _____

  _____

  _____

  _____

  - Did you incorporate any mental exercises, like positive affirmations or visualization?

  _____

  _____

  _____

  _____

  _____

  - How did you make sure you were physically ready? Did you engage in a warm-up or light exercise?

  _____

  _____

_____

_____

_____

- **Assess your total routine:**

  - Review everything you've written. How thorough was your preparation?

_____

_____

_____

_____

_____

  - Did you make choices that helped optimize your performance on and off the field?

_____

_____

_____

_____

_____

  - What improvements can you make for the next game?

_____

_____

_____

_____

_____

By engaging in this exercise, you're taking important steps toward becoming a more mindful and prepared athlete! Remember, preparation begins the night before, and every detail counts in helping you perform your best.

Bringing It Home

Throughout this chapter, we've looked at ways to build team chemistry by recognizing everyone's unique strengths and offering valuable feedback that encourages growth.

Implementing the strategies within this chapter can set the foundation for personal and team success. Keep practicing these skills and you'll not only become a better teammate but also a confident leader, ready to take on whatever the game throws your way!

Chapter 7: Motivation—Finding Your Why

I think self-awareness is probably the most important thing towards being a champion. —Billie Jean King

Motivation is about understanding the deeper reasons behind why you lace up your cleats and hit the field day after day. It's not merely for the sake of winning or being the top player; it's much more personal and fulfilling than that. Discovering your why can change how you view practices, games, and even the challenges that come your way. This chapter looks into identifying what truly drives you and how connecting with this motivation can bring enthusiasm and dedication into every part of your softball experience.

In this chapter, you'll explore strategies for uncovering your personal motivations and see how they can become friends in your journey through sports. It's time to find ways to fuel your passion for softball, making each practice and game more meaningful.

Discovering Your Personal Motivation for Playing Softball

Discovering what truly drives you to play softball can change everything. It's about finding that spark that gets you out of bed and onto the field with enthusiasm. For many, it's not just about winning games or being the best player on the team; it's about the joy and excitement that comes with every swing of the bat and every catch.

Understanding Your Passion

First off, think about what excites you most about softball. Is it the adrenaline rush during a close game? The togetherness of working with teammates? Or maybe the satisfaction of improving after hours of practice? Each player's source of excitement can vary. Understanding these elements helps you stay committed even when the going gets tough. If making that perfect pitch or nailing that home run fills you with thrill, then that's something to focus on and nurture. Commitment in any sport is linked directly to the enjoyment of playing.

Identifying Personal Values

Connecting personal values to your reasons for playing is also important in strengthening satisfaction and resilience. Your values act as guiding stars—they help steer your path and decisions on the field. Maybe you value teamwork and the collaboration needed to achieve common goals. Or perhaps it's about pushing boundaries and challenging yourself. By aligning these values with your participation in softball, you create a deeper sense of purpose, changing the experience into something far more meaningful than just a pastime.

Personal satisfaction increases when there's value alignment because you're doing something that resonates with who you are. For example, if you deeply value persistence and see that mirrored in your daily practices and efforts to improve, each win, regardless of size, becomes so satisfying. This connection works wonders for building resilience. When personal values drive your motivation, setbacks become mere building blocks rather than roadblocks, empowering you to bounce back with renewed motivation.

Reflecting on Influential Moments

Reflecting on past influential moments can also bring together a compelling personal story. Think back to those pivotal times that shaped your journey in softball. It could be a memory of watching a thrilling game that inspired you to pick up a bat or perhaps a moment when someone famous in the sport made an impact on you. Recalling these experiences helps in crafting a narrative that motivates you today. These stories are powerful reminders of why you started and how far you've come. They remind you of the obstacles you've overcome and the determination that fueled your progress.

These kinds of reflections create a sense of identity as an athlete. You start seeing yourself not just as someone who plays softball but as a key part of its strong community. Your story becomes a testament to hard work, dedication, and continuous growth. It serves to inspire not only you but also others around you who might be starting down similar paths. Accepting and owning your unique story strengthens your mental game by providing a source of intrinsic motivation that remains unwavering in face-offs and challenges.

To illustrate, say there was a time when you felt like giving up, maybe due to a series of losses or a prolonged slump in form. But then, revisiting a past success or even just remembering how much you love the sport helped you push through. These incidents provide strength and confidence to tackle future challenges head-on by reinforcing the belief that you have done it before and can certainly do it again.

How Motivation Impacts Your Attitude and Performance

Motivation is the driving force that powers athletes on the field, and its influence stretches far beyond just physical performance. When you understand what lights your fire, it becomes a lot easier to approach softball with a positive mindset. You'll even find yourself becoming more enthusiastic and determined, pushing you to give your best, even when things get tough. That can push you to give your best, even when things get tough.

Positive Attitude and Performance Link

Every game and every practice session offers a chance to learn and grow. Yet, without motivation, the regular grind can feel like a chore. Motivation helps you see each practice as a step toward improvement rather than just another job. Having that internal drive makes you more likely to show up day after day, ready to put in the work. Consistency in practice leads to skill improvement, making you a formidable player over time.

Research also tells us that athletes who believe in their abilities are more driven. For them, everything revolves around their sport, creating a central focus that guides their daily decisions and efforts (Karageorghis, 2023). This commitment is a testament to how motivation can define your journey, turning aspirations into realities through relentless dedication.

Mental Toughness Development

In competitive sports like softball, mental toughness is vital. It's about staying focused, confident, and in control under pressure. Motivation plays a crucial role in developing this toughness. The desire to succeed keeps you mentally engaged, helping you tackle competition strategies head-on. When you're driven, you're better at coping with both expected and unforeseen challenges. Research highlights that mental toughness correlates strongly with success, not just in terms of winning games but also in maintaining psychological well-being (The Role of Mental Toughness in Sport Performance, 2018).

A motivated athlete often sets personal goals that align with both intrinsic and extrinsic motives. This balance helps sustain motivation over the long haul (Karageorghis, 2023).

Intrinsic motivation is when you do something because you enjoy it or because it makes you feel good inside. It's about the fun and satisfaction you get from softball itself, not because you're trying to get something like a prize or a reward.

Extrinsic motivation is when you do something to get something in return, like a trophy, medal, or praise. It's about doing the activity because of the rewards outside of the activity itself.

A softball player's love for the game should ideally spring from both the enjoyment of competing and the satisfaction of improving themselves. It's about finding your why, the reason you keep striving for excellence. Motivation turns dreams into plans and plans into triumphs.

Your Softball Story & Purpose

Guidelines:

- Spend 15-20 minutes writing freely

- Be specific with examples

- Focus on feelings and personal meaning

- Review your answers periodically to stay connected with your motivation

Part 1: Core Questions

What moment first sparked your love for softball? Describe it in detail.

_____

_____

_____

_____

_____

When do you feel most alive on the field? What specific aspects of the game bring you joy?

_____

_____

_____

_____

_____

Think of your toughest moment in softball. What made you continue despite the challenge?

_____

_____

_____

_____

_____

How does softball align with your personal values? (Examples: teamwork, perseverance, excellence)

_____

_____

_____

_____

Part 2: Impact & Growth

How has softball shaped who you are today?

_____

_____

_____

_____

_____

What impact do you want to have on your team and the sport?

_____

_____

_____

_____

Beyond winning, what do you want to achieve through softball?

_____

_____

_____

_____

_____

How Pre-Game Routines Help With Focus and Consistency

Creating a sense of control is key for athletes when approaching a game. Pre-game routines provide a structured way to manage nerves and reduce uncertainties, which ultimately decreases anxiety. Imagine stepping onto the field already knowing what your next moves will be—that's the power of a well-established routine. Athletes are often faced with unpredictable scenarios during games. By having a set pre-game ritual, you establish a routine that prepares you mentally and physically, allowing you to focus on the game rather than being overwhelmed by the unexpected.

Taking control can come from simple steps:

- Warming up in a particular order.

- Listening to a specific playlist.

- Using visualization techniques to mentally rehearse game scenarios.

Batters can't control where the pitch is going to go, or where the defense is positioned, and so forth. But they can control their swing or the pitch they swing at. Batters can also control how prepared they are and their attitude.

Pitchers can't control the batters or if the defense is going to make the play. But they can control their emotions, attitude, and preparedness.

Focusing on what you can control is very important in softball.

Enhancing Mental Focus

Enhancing mental focus through intentional activities is another vital component of pre-game routines. Mindfulness exercises play a key role here, helping athletes stay present and focused. Things like mindful breathing or simply taking a moment to center yourself can improve your attentiveness. According to research, mindfulness helps young athletes stay engaged during competitions and training sessions (Broadway, 2023). Exercises such as visualization, where you picture yourself successfully executing plays, build confidence and develop a winning mindset. These mindful activities channel all your energy into the present moment, making it easier to perform under pressure.

Establishing Consistency

Consistency is key to success in any sport, and pre-game routines create this trait in athletes. Familiar practices become second nature, which boosts execution even under high-pressure situations. For softball players, this might mean repeating a warm-up sequence until it feels instinctual. Once these routines are ingrained, they boost performance metrics because your body learns what to expect and how to react.

Consistently following a structured routine makes transitioning from preparation to action smoother. The habit of consistency extends beyond physical routines; it affects mental readiness, too, preparing you to tackle challenges head-on without hesitation.

Personalization of Routines

An important aspect of creating effective pre-game routines is personalization. Not everyone finds the same methods effective, so tailoring activities to suit individual preferences can make them more engaging and beneficial. A personalized routine reflects what truly energizes and prepares you for a game. Whether it's a specific type of music, motivational mantras, or unique stretches, discovering what works best for you adds value to the experience and increases its effectiveness. Personalization means taking ownership of your routine, crafting something uniquely tailored to optimize your mental and emotional state.

Think of pre-game routines as your secret weapon—a tailored strategy designed to get you in the zone. Every athlete has different needs and preferences, so customizing your approach can elevate your pre-game experience. Incorporating elements that resonate personally can make the routine enjoyable and something you look forward to. Engaging in something meaningful before a game primes your mind and body for success.

Bringing It Home

In this chapter, we've explored how discovering your personal motivation can totally change your game and fuel your passion for softball. It's not just about hitting home runs or winning—it's about understanding what truly excites you.

By establishing pre-game habits, like listening to your favorite music or visualizing game scenarios, you're prepping yourself for success. Personalizing these routines ensures they fit you perfectly, making every game something to look forward to. Remember, both motivation and routine are keys to unlocking consistent improvement and fun in softball, giving you the edge to shine on the field.

Chapter 8: Dealing With Pressure—Handling Expectations

Try not to get lost in comparing yourself to others. Discover your gifts and let them shine! – Jennie Finch

Dealing with pressure is a major part of playing sports. It's something all athletes encounter—from the expectations set by coaches and parents to those that come from within. Understanding how different types of pressure affect your performance is key. Learning how to identify constructive feedback versus unrealistic demands is essential for any athlete wanting to excel without feeling overwhelmed. In this chapter, we'll explore how to walk the tightrope between helpful guidance and harmful stress, whether it comes from those watching you play or from your own high standards.

Throughout the pages ahead, you'll find practical advice and techniques tailored for young athletes like yourself. By the end of the chapter, you'll have a toolkit of methods to tackle pressure head-on, turning challenges into opportunities for growth in both your sport and life.

Handling External and Internal Pressure

Dealing with pressure is a big part of the game. Athletes often face expectations from their coaches, parents, teammates, *and* themselves. Understanding the difference between feedback that helps you grow and unrealistic expectations that can hurt your performance is crucial. Coaches and parents usually want to see you succeed, but sometimes their words may feel like too much pressure. It's important to recognize when their advice is meant to help you improve versus when you might be perceiving it as an expectation to always perform perfectly.

For example, if a coach advises you on improving your swing in softball, this is helpful feedback designed to boost your skills. However, incorrectly interpreting this advice as a demand for perfection can increase stress levels unnecessarily. According to research, managing these pressures effectively means learning to see the difference between constructive guidance and undue expectations (Endo et al., 2023). Recognizing where the pressure comes from helps you handle it better and maintain a positive attitude toward your sport.

Identifying Internal Pressure

Self-imposed personal goals can also cause internal pressure, leading to anxiety and performance struggles. Setting high goals isn't inherently bad, but they need to be realistic and attainable. Unrealistic objectives, like expecting to hit a home run every game, can set you up for disappointment and affect your confidence. When you establish achievable goals, you create a sense of accomplishment that fuels your motivation and reduces anxiety.

To manage this, try breaking down your larger objectives into smaller, manageable tasks. This way, you're consistently working toward your bigger goal while celebrating the smaller wins that help keep your spirits high.

Balancing Expectations

Another important aspect of handling pressure is adopting a process-focused mindset. Many athletes get caught up in results and outcomes, such as winning games or scoring points. While winning is rewarding, only emphasizing outcomes can amplify stress, especially if things don't go as planned. Instead, shift your focus to enjoying the journey of improvement—the practices, the strategies, and the teamwork involved in becoming better at your sport.

Think about your favorite professional athlete. Now, remember that they didn't achieve greatness by winning every match but by dedicating themselves to practicing, learning, and growing through challenges. Similarly, by valuing the process over immediate results, you lessen the burden of expectations and open yourself up to learning from both wins and losses. This balanced approach helps align your ambitions with what's realistically achievable, building a healthier relationship with your sport.

Exercise: Balancing Expectations for Softball Athletes
Objective: To help you understand and balance different expectations while maintaining a positive mindset and focusing on the process.

Instructions:

- **Identifying expectations**

    - In each section, write down the expectations you feel coming from yourself, your coaches, and your teammates or peers. Be honest and specific.

Personal Expectations

Coaches Expectations

Team/Peer Expectations

- Reflect on how these expectations make you feel. Do they motivate you, or do they cause stress?

_____

_____

_____

_____

_____

- **Finding the middle ground**

○ Look at the expectations you've listed and write down any overlaps or common themes between them.

_____

_____

_____

_____

_____

○ Write down one or two personal goals that align with both your ambitions and the expectations of others. For example, "I want to improve my batting average while also being a supportive teammate."

_____

_____

_____

_____

_____

○ Visualize how achieving these goals can satisfy both your needs and those of your coaches and teammates.

- **Clarifying communication**

  ○ Consider discussing your expectations with your coaches and teammates. Write down key points you want to express, such as:

    ■ Your goals and aspirations.

_____

_____

_____

_____

_____

    ■ How you're feeling about the expectations placed on you.

_____

_____

_____

_____

_____

    ■ Ways they can support you in achieving your goals.

_____

- Practice this conversation with a friend or family member or just in front of a mirror to build confidence.

- If you aren't comfortable talking to your coaches, you can write it on a piece of paper and hand it to them before or after practice.

- **Mindset shifts**

  - Write down a specific performance goal you have (e.g., "I want to hit a home run") and recognize the pressure that comes with it.

_____

  - Shift your focus to the process: List out the steps you need to take to achieve this goal (e.g., practice hitting techniques, improving footwork, getting feedback from coaches).

_____

  - Each time you feel stressed about the outcome, remind yourself of your commitment to the process, celebrating the small progress along the way.

- **Reflect and check-in**

  - Schedule a weekly check-in with yourself to reflect on how you're managing expectations. Ask yourself:

    - Am I feeling balanced?

_____
_____
_____
_____
_____

- What strategies are helping me?

_____
_____
_____
_____
_____

- Do I need to communicate any changes in my goals or needs?

_____
_____
_____
_____
_____

○ Consider sharing your experience with a trusted teammate or coach for support and encouragement.

Balancing expectations from all sources is key to maintaining a positive mindset in softball. By actively communicating, focusing on the process, and setting personal goals, you'll build resilience and enjoy your athletic journey!

Constructive Pressure

While external pressures are common, recognizing them can give you control over how they impact your performance. Different kinds of pressures exist during matches and practices. Some occur unintentionally, like the sense of responsibility you feel due to your position on the team. Others are intentional, such as a coach setting challenging training sessions to prepare you for real-game scenarios. Both types are designed to ultimately boost your abilities, but understanding them helps you know which pressures to accept and which ones to alleviate.

Talking to your coach, teammates, or family members about what you're feeling can provide relief and perspective. It's okay to express when certain expectations feel overwhelming. Open communication creates a supportive environment where everyone can thrive rather than buckle under silent stress.

Develop a Pressure Release Technique

Handling pressure during competitions is a skill that can be developed with the right techniques and consistent practice. For young athletes, particularly those involved in sports like softball, learning to manage stress can boost performance in a big way. Let's take a look at methods such as deep breathing, visualization, and grounding exercises that can help you deal with pressure effectively.

- **Deep breathing:** When you focus on slow, controlled breaths, you can reduce anxiety and bring your heart rate down during tense moments. This simple technique shifts attention from anxiety-triggering thoughts to the rhythm of breathing, creating a calming effect. To practice, find a quiet spot before a game or even during breaks, close your eyes, and take a deep breath through your nose. Hold it for a few seconds, then exhale slowly through your mouth. That's it! Repeat this process several times until you feel calmer and more focused.

- **Visualization:** We've talked about how visualization involves mentally rehearsing a successful performance. You simply imagine yourself executing plays perfectly. This can include hitting a home run or making a difficult catch. It's about seeing every detail—how you move, how the ball feels against the bat, and hearing the cheer of the crowd. According to Straw (2024), visualizing positive outcomes helps in building confidence and preparing the mind for actual gameplay. Make this part of your routine before every match. Find a quiet place where you won't be disturbed, close your eyes, and visualize every step of your performance. The more detailed your visualization, the better prepared you'll feel when you're on the field.

- **Grounding:** Grounding exercises are essential, especially when feelings of anxiety or panic begin to set in. Grounding techniques involve bringing yourself back to the present moment by using physical sensations. One simple method is the 5-4-3-2-1 exercise: Identify five things you can see, four things you can touch, three things you can hear, two things you can smell, and one thing you can taste. This exercise helps shift focus away from pressure-inducing thoughts and anchors you in reality, reducing anxiety. Nortje (2020) emphasizes grounding as a way to maintain awareness and control over one's reactions to stressful situations.

Consistency is key when blending these techniques into your routine. Practicing them regularly before competitions can boost their effectiveness when under pressure. Just like any skill, the more you practice, the more natural it becomes. Use these exercises in daily practices and workouts—not just on game day. Doing so will condition your body and mind to respond automatically to high-pressure scenarios, improving your overall performance.

To maximize these techniques, create a personalized plan that incorporates specific strategies for different high-pressure scenarios. Consider situations that make you anxious during competitions. Is it hitting under pressure? Making a crucial play? Tailor your plans to address these challenges. Start by writing down each scenario, then choose which technique fits best. For instance, if you tend to get anxious while waiting to bat, use deep breathing. If you're nervous about executing a particular play, visualize successfully completing it beforehand. With practice, these personalized strategies become second nature, allowing you to remain calm and focused no matter what pressures arise during the game.

Exercise: Understanding Pressure Release Techniques for Softball Athletes

Objective: To help you explore and practice different pressure-release techniques that can be used to manage anxiety and boost performance during competitions.

Deep Breathing With Color Visualization
- Find a quiet place to sit or stand comfortably.

- Close your eyes, if you want, and take three deep breaths, inhaling through your nose and exhaling through your mouth.

- As you breathe in, imagine a calming color, like blue or green, filling your body, representing calmness. Hold that color in your mind.

- As you exhale, visualize a darker color, like gray or brown, representing the stress or pressure leaving your body.

- Repeat this process for five breaths, focusing on the colors and how your body feels.

Success Memory Visualization
- Sit comfortably and close your eyes if that feels comfortable. Take a deep breath to relax.

- Think of a time when you felt successful in softball—maybe a great hit, catch, or any moment when you felt proud.

- Visualize this scene in detail: where you were, the sounds around you, how you felt in that moment.

- Imagine achieving that success again, focusing on the feelings of confidence and joy.

- Practice this visualization regularly, especially before big games, to remind yourself of your capabilities.

Grounding Exercise With Five Senses

- Stand or sit comfortably, and take a few deep breaths.

- Use your senses to ground yourself in the present moment:

    - **Sight:** Look around and notice five things you can see. Describe them in your mind.

    - **Touch:** Focus on four things you can feel (the ground beneath your feet, your glove, your heartbeat).

    - **Hearing:** Listen for three sounds (the wind, laughter, or nature around you).

    - **Smell:** Identify two positive scents (grass, a flower).

    - **Taste:** Focus on one taste (like a sip of water or gum).

- This exercise helps you stay anchored and focused, reducing anxiety.

"Warrior Pose" Physical Release

- Stand tall with your feet hip-width apart. Take a deep breath in and raise your arms overhead.

- As you exhale, step your left foot back into a lunge, bending your right knee while keeping your arms lifted.

- Hold this warrior pose for a few breaths, channeling strength and confidence.

- Switch sides, stepping back with your right foot and holding the pose again. Feel the power of your body grounding you.

- Repeat this several times, using it as a physical way to release tension and embrace strength.

Experimentation and Reflection

- Over the next week, practice each of these techniques and pay attention to how they make you feel.

- Keep a journal to note which techniques resonate most with you and when you find them most useful (e.g., before practice, during a game, or after a mistake).

- Reflect on how these techniques impact your performance and mindset, and be open to trying new methods as you grow.

Exploring different pressure release techniques can greatly enhance your ability to manage stress and perform well in softball. By regularly practicing these unique methods, you'll discover what works best for you and build a strong toolkit for success on and off the field!

Identifying Signs of Stress and How to Manage Them

In the world of competitive sports, understanding stress signals is like learning a new pitch, it takes practice but makes all the difference. Most likely, you often juggle the pressures of performance with everyday life stressors. These stressors can lead to both physical symptoms, like headaches or fatigue, and emotional ones, such as anxiety or irritability. Recognizing these signals early can make a big difference in managing them effectively. It's crucial for you to pay attention to changes in your body and mood. Consider keeping a journal to track these signals; this simple tool can help you identify patterns and triggers, making it easier to develop proactive strategies.

Coping Strategies

Self-care isn't just a buzzword—it's your game plan off the field. According to research, practicing self-care routines can fend off burnout and mental health issues among elite athletes (Drummond, 2023). Simple adjustments like ensuring adequate sleep, balanced nutrition, and incorporating regular relaxation activities, such as meditation or yoga, can act as preventive measures against stress. For instance, scheduling regular downtime in your week can be as crucial as a practice session, letting your mind recharge and refocus. Additionally, engaging in hobbies outside the sport is vital as these activities provide mental breaks and keep life balanced.

Creating a Support Network

Having an open line of communication with a support network can greatly improve your resilience against stress. Building connections with those who understand and respect the unique challenges you face is essential. This network may include family, friends, teammates, and notably, coaches. Coaches aren't just there to guide on physical performance; they can be incredible allies in managing mental health.

Bringing It Home

Managing expectations and stress helps you not just survive but thrive under pressure in competitive sports. You've seen how recognizing different types of pressures—whether they come from coaches, parents, or your own goals—is the first step in handling them effectively. It's key to distinguish between helpful guidance and unrealistic expectations that can weigh you down.

The importance of stress management techniques cannot be overstated. From deep breathing and visualization to grounding exercises, these tools help you stay focused and calm under pressure. Take advantage of these strategies to manage stress constructively and take charge of your athletic journey, turning every challenge into an opportunity for growth and self-improvement.

Chapter 9: Accountability—Taking Responsibility for Your Growth

Never limit yourself, never be satisfied, and smile; it's free! –Jennie Finch

Taking responsibility for your growth means embracing accountability. It's not just about what happens on the field but how you respond to it, learn from it, and build upon it. Accountability allows you to take ownership of both your successes and setbacks, which is an essential part of personal development.

In this chapter, you'll take a closer look into the role accountability plays in boosting performance and personal growth. By accepting accountability, this chapter aims to equip you with practical tools and insights to elevate your mental game, helping you thrive in softball and any other sport or challenge life throws your way.

The Importance of Accountability in Personal and Athletic Growth

Let's talk about something that might not always be at the forefront of your training but is super important for both your personal growth and your success on the softball field: accountability. It's a big word, but let's break it down and see how it can help you level up your game!

Defining Accountability

So, what does accountability really mean in sports? It's all about taking ownership of your actions and performances. When you hold yourself accountable, you recognize that what you do, whether in practice or during a game, has a direct impact on your success and on the success of your team. Think about it: When everyone takes responsibility for their individual efforts, the whole team shines brighter! And hey, when mistakes happen (and they will), taking responsibility helps you learn and grow. It changes how you view those moments. Instead of seeing failure, you see a chance to become better.

Benefits of Accountability

So, what are the benefits? When you embrace accountability, you're setting yourself up for consistent improvement. Being accountable means you're open to feedback, which is essential for growth. Imagine how awesome it feels when everyone on your team respects each other and you're all helping one another out. That environment of mutual respect can really boost your performance and motivation.

Strategies for Building Accountability

Ready to put accountability into action? Here are some practical strategies to make it happen:

- **Self-monitoring practices:** Keep track of your progress. Jot down your goals and reflect on your daily performances. Seeing how far you've come can be incredibly motivating and keeps you accountable to yourself.

- **Set benchmarks:** Create specific milestones for your performance and check in on them regularly. This proactive mindset helps you stay focused and gives you clear targets to strive for.

- **Open communication:** Don't hesitate to talk with your coaches and teammates about your goals and challenges. Sharing your thoughts fosters a culture of accountability, making it easier for everyone to support one another.

Remember, accountability is more than just a word; it's a game-changer for how you approach softball and life. Own your journey, and watch how it transforms not only your performance but also your personal growth. Keep pushing forward!

Exercise: Building Accountability in Softball

Objective: To help you develop personal accountability through self-monitoring, goal setting, and communication.

Part 1: Self-Monitoring Practices
- **Goal setting:** Write down three specific goals you want to achieve over the next month (e.g., improving batting average, enhancing fielding skills, or increasing stamina).

- o Goal 1: _____

- o Goal 2: _____

- o Goal 3: _____

- **Daily reflection journal:** At the end of each practice, spend 5 minutes reflecting on your performance. Answer the following questions:

  - o What did I do well today?

  _____
  _____
  _____
  _____
  _____
  _____
  _____

  - o What do I need to improve upon?

  _____
  _____
  _____
  _____
  _____
  _____
  _____

  - o How did I hold myself accountable to my goals?

  _____
  _____
  _____
  _____
  _____
  _____
  _____

Part 2: Setting Benchmarks

- **Create benchmarks:** Establish measurable benchmarks for each of your goals. For example:

  - o For batting average improvement, set a benchmark of reaching a specific percentage by the end of each week.

- For fielding skills, aim to make a certain number of successful catches during practice each week.

- Benchmark for goal 1: _____

- Benchmark for goal 2: _____

- Benchmark for goal 3: _____

- **Weekly evaluation:** At the end of each week, evaluate your progress toward your benchmarks. Write a summary of your performance:

  - What progress did I make?

_____
_____
_____
_____
_____
_____
_____
_____
_____
_____
_____
_____

  - What challenges did I encounter?

_____
_____
_____
_____
_____
_____
_____
_____
_____
_____
_____

  - What adjustments do I need to make for next week?

_____
_____

_____
_____
_____
_____
_____
_____
_____
_____
_____

_____

Part 3: Open Communication

- **Team meetings:** Organize a weekly team meeting to discuss progress on goals and benchmarks. Use the following prompts to guide your discussion:

  ○ How are my teammates progressing with their individual goals?

  _____
  _____
  _____
  _____
  _____

  ○ What positive accountability strategies have worked well for my team?

  _____
  _____
  _____
  _____
  _____

  ○ How can we support each other in achieving our goals?

  _____
  _____
  _____
  _____
  _____

- **Check-ins with coaches:** Schedule one-on-one check-ins with your coach to discuss your goals and progress. Prepare questions you want to ask:

  ○ What feedback do you have on my performance?

  ○ How can I improve accountability for myself?

Reflection

After completing these exercises over a month, reflect on your experience:

- How has building accountability changed your approach to softball?

_____
_____
_____
_____
_____
_____
_____
_____
_____
_____
_____
_____

- What strategies worked best for you?

_____
_____
_____
_____
_____
_____
_____
_____
_____
_____
_____
_____

- What goals do you want to set for the next month?

_____
_____
_____
_____
_____
_____
_____

_____
_____
_____

By consistently practicing these strategies, you will strengthen your personal accountability, enhance your performance, and create a supportive team culture that encourages everyone to excel!

And let's not forget the importance of maintaining a balance between creativity and accountability. Sports encourage creativity—just think of the innovative plays in softball or the unexpected moves that surprise opponents. However, without accountability, creativity could lead to chaos. Setting boundaries and understanding responsibilities ensures that creative energy is channeled in the right direction, ultimately leading to progress.

How to Accept Feedback and Use It for Improvement

Taking responsibility for your growth as an athlete is a powerful step to achieving your goals. Learning how to receive feedback constructively is essential because, when approached positively, it can be the key to unlocking your full potential.

Understanding Feedback

Understanding the difference between constructive criticism and negative comments is crucial. Constructive criticism is meant to help you improve—it's specific, actionable, and focused on aspects you can change. Negative comments, however, often lack specific guidance and may focus more on personal traits rather than performance. Being able to tell the difference helps you concentrate on practical improvements rather than getting bogged down by non-constructive remarks.

Active Listening Skills

Active listening is key in how feedback is received. This skill involves giving full attention to the speaker, making eye contact, and responding appropriately. By practicing active listening, you guarantee that you fully understand the feedback they're receiving. It also shows respect and openness, which can encourage coaches or teammates to provide honest and helpful advice. To boost these skills, you should try summarizing what you heard and ask questions if anything's unclear.

Implementing Feedback

Once feedback is clearly understood through active listening, the next step is implementing this feedback by setting specific goals. Goals give direction to how you can use the advice. Remember to break down large pieces of feedback into smaller, manageable tasks. When you set clear, achievable objectives, you create a proactive approach to improvement. For instance, if a coach points out that you need to improve your batting stance, you might set a goal to practice specific drills that strengthen this aspect every week. That way, you turn feedback into real action steps that steadily lead to growth and better performance.

Sharing Feedback

Promoting mutual feedback among teammates is another effective strategy. When you create a culture where giving and receiving feedback is normalized, it strengthens team dynamics and personal accountability. Encouraging peer feedback allows you to gain insights from different perspectives and supports a collaborative environment. This type of exchange builds trust and improves the overall team atmosphere, so everyone feels valued and invested in each other's progress. As the team becomes accustomed to both providing and receiving feedback regularly, they build a stronger sense of community and open communication within the team.

Write Down One Area of Your Game Where You Want to Improve

Let's take a moment to dive into a really important topic: improvement. Whether you're a powerhouse pitcher or a fierce outfielder, there's always something you can work on to take your game to the next level.

Self-Reflection Practices

First up, let's talk about self-reflection. This is all about being honest with yourself about where you're at in your game. It might feel a little tough at first, but regularly assessing your performance will help you figure out your strengths and weaknesses. Try journaling about specific experiences during practices or games. Was there a play that didn't go as planned? Or maybe a moment when you felt on top of your game? Writing these down can help you spot patterns and recurring challenges, making it easier to identify areas for improvement. And don't forget to set aside time for self-assessment! Even just a few minutes a week can make a huge difference in your focused development.

Setting Improvement Goals

Once you've pinpointed an area you want to improve, it's time to set some actionable goals. For example, if you want to work on your batting, you might set a goal to increase your batting average by a certain percentage over the season. This kind of targeted practice helps keep you accountable. Remember to define clear criteria for success—it'll help keep you motivated as you tackle those weaknesses. Don't forget to check in on your goals regularly and adjust them as you grow to stay adaptable.

Creating an Improvement Plan

Now, let's craft an effective game improvement plan. Break down those larger goals into smaller, more manageable steps. This makes everything feel less overwhelming and more achievable. Don't hesitate to lean on your support system. Coaches, teammates, and mentors can be fantastic for providing guidance and encouragement throughout your journey. Establishing timelines for your goals creates a little urgency and keeps you committed to your plan.

Tracking Progress

Lastly, let's talk about tracking your progress. Keeping a record of your challenges and the milestones you've reached is super motivating. Celebrate those small wins! Each little win adds up and builds your confidence. Periodic reviews of your progress will help you see what needs further attention and adjustments.

Remember, improvement is a journey, not a destination. Embrace the process, cheer yourself on, and watch as you elevate your game one step at a time. You've got this!

Exercise: Tracking Progress in Softball

Objective: To help you understand the importance of documenting your progress, celebrating achievements, and identifying areas for improvement.

Part 1: Documenting Progress

- **Progress journal:** Start a dedicated softball progress journal. Each week, write down:

  - Date: _____

  - Practice focus (e.g., hitting, fielding, conditioning):
    _____

  - Key takeaways from practice:
    _____
    _____
    _____

  - Challenges faced:
    _____
    _____
    _____

- **Milestones checklist:** Create a list of milestones you want to achieve this season (e.g., completing a certain number of successful plays, achieving a specific batting average, etc.). Check them off as you accomplish each milestone.

  - Milestone 1: _____

  - Milestone 2: _____

  - Milestone 3: _____

Part 2: Celebrating Small Victories

- **Victory log:** Every time you achieve a goal or overcome a challenge, document it in your progress journal.

  - Date: _____

○ Achievement: _____

○ How it made you feel:

_____

_____

- **Reward yourself:** Create a personal reward system. Decide on small rewards for reaching specific milestones (e.g., treating yourself to ice cream, a new piece of gear, or a fun outing with friends). Write down your rewards:

  ○ Reward for Milestone 1: _____

  ○ Reward for Milestone 2: _____

  ○ Reward for Milestone 3: _____

Part 3: Periodic Reviews

- **Weekly review sessions:** At the end of each week, sit down and review your journal entries.

  ○ Progress: What improvements did you make?

_____

_____

_____

_____

_____

  ○ Challenges: What obstacles did you face?

_____

_____

_____

_____

_____

  ○ Adjustments: What changes can you make to continue improving?

_____

_____

_____

_____

_____

- **Coach feedback:** Share your progress journal with your coach during one-on-one meetings.

  - Your achievements and any areas where you need assistance.

  - Strategies to work on challenges you're facing.

Reflection

At the end of the season, look back at your progress journal and reflect on the following:

- What were your biggest accomplishments?

_____
_____
_____
_____
_____
_____
_____
_____
_____
_____
_____
_____

- How did documenting your progress motivate you?

_____
_____
_____
_____
_____
_____
_____
_____
_____
_____
_____

- What areas do you still want to work on in the future?

_____
_____
_____
_____

Bringing It Home

Owning accountability and learning from feedback are stepping stones to personal growth, especially in sports like softball. Throughout this chapter, we've explored how taking responsibility for actions on the field can elevate both individual and team performance.

Whether you're a pitcher aiming to strengthen your fastball or a batter seeking better reaction time, breaking down feedback into achievable steps encourages growth. By embracing accountability and feedback as tools for improvement, you build resilience, strengthen your mental game, and create a supportive team environment.

Chapter 10: Owning Your Success and Recognizing Progress

Success is a project that's always under construction. —Pat Summitt

Owning your success and recognizing progress is all about giving yourself the credit you deserve as you hit milestones, both big and small. It's easy to overlook these moments when you're constantly aiming for something greater in competitive sports like softball. But imagine how empowering it feels when you finally connect perfectly with the bat or outsmart an opposing player with a calculated play. This chapter dives deep into why acknowledging each step forward boosts your mental game.

By the end of this chapter, you'll have a toolkit of techniques to help recognize progress effectively, creating both personal and collective growth.

Acknowledging Both Big and Small Achievements

Recognizing that all achievements contribute to your growth and confidence is crucial for developing a positive mindset, especially in competitive sports like softball. Often, athletes focus so intensely on their end goals that they overlook their smaller successes along the way. These achievements, however minor they seem, are essential steps in building self-belief and motivation.

Understanding Achievements

Understanding achievements starts with acknowledging every victory, no matter how tiny, to help you see progress in your journey. For instance, even if it's just improving your batting average slightly or mastering a new training routine, each achievement signifies your commitment and dedication. According to BookBaker (2024), recognizing these small successes helps build positivity, allowing you to maintain enthusiasm and resilience. Appreciating these wins further encourages you to keep pushing toward those larger goals.

Creating Success Logs

Creating a success log is a practical way to track and reflect on these achievements. This method provides a visual record of your progress and can be a powerful source of motivation. Consider keeping a journal where you jot down daily wins, like making it through a tough practice session or executing a new technique perfectly. That way, you can revisit past victories, reminding yourself of how far you've come.

To start a success log, get a notebook or use an app where you can easily input your daily wins. At the end of each week or month, review these notes and reflect on the progress you've made. Doing this consistently not only boosts your morale but also reinforces the habit of focusing on the positive aspects of your efforts. It highlights areas of improvement and sheds light on patterns that might need more attention, guiding you to make well-informed adjustments to your training routine.

Embracing Milestones

Embracing milestones offers exciting opportunities for celebration and recognizing the significance of key moments in your journey. They could be specific achievements like winning a game, being selected as team captain, or reaching a personal best. Celebrating acknowledges the hard work involved and marks important checkpoints on your path. When you welcome these moments, you allow yourself to pause, appreciate, and renew your energy for future challenges.

Consider organizing small celebrations with your teammates when someone reaches a milestone. Whether it's a pizza party after a win or posting about it online, these acknowledgments strengthen team bonds and boost individual spirits.

Reflection on Achievements

By analyzing what led to these accolades, you can identify strategies and techniques that worked well. Reflecting on a milestone, like pitching a perfect game, lets you understand the preparation and mental state necessary for such accomplishments. This reflection equips you with insights that can be applied to future endeavors, reinforcing the cycle of continuous improvement and growth.

In essence, recognizing all achievements is vital for nurturing a positive mindset and boosting confidence. By regularly acknowledging both big and small successes, you build mental storage of positivity and resilience that fuels your journey in sports and beyond. Creating a success log not only keeps you motivated but also serves as a real testament to your dedication and effort. Embracing milestones further celebrates your progress and provides invaluable lessons for future challenges.

How Celebrating Progress Helps Build Confidence and Motivation

Imagine when you score a winning run or finally master that tricky pitch you've been practicing; taking a moment to celebrate these wins affects your mind positively. Celebrations reinforce successful behaviors and boost what psychologists call "self-efficacy," which is basically believing you can achieve what you set out to do (Cherry, 2024).

Successful Mindset Building

Think of it like this: every celebration is like adding a new brick to the fortress of your self-belief. It nudges your brain to remember that you've done something awesome and reminds you that you can repeat those successes. Celebrating is like telling yourself, "Hey, I've got this!" This belief doesn't just make you feel good temporarily—it builds a mindset that can handle challenges with more courage.

Instead of waiting for big wins, recognize the importance of smaller milestones too. Maybe it's improving your throwing speed or nailing a complex team play. Each celebration helps instill resilience—a crucial aspect of developing a growth mindset that says you can keep learning and growing, no matter what obstacles come your way.

Creating a Celebration Ritual

Now, let's talk about creating celebration rituals to structure these positive reinforcements. A ritual can be as simple as a team high-five circle after a game or sharing highlights from practice over your favorite ice cream. These rituals offer structure, making celebrations part of your routine rather than just an occasional event. They add a sense of fun, making hard work seem more rewarding. When everyone gets to share in the joy of achievements together, it drastically boosts team bonding. When teammates celebrate each other's victories, individual confidence shoots up because everyone feels supported and appreciated. To get started, consider setting up a quick post-game huddle where everyone names one thing they did well. This way, you'll not only establish a tradition but also encourage continuous reflection on progress and success.

Feedback Loop

An interesting feedback loop exists between performance and celebration. When you perform well, you celebrate, which in turn motivates you for future performances. Let's say your team wins a tough match. You celebrate the pride and joy of that win, which acts as a motivational booster, fueling your desire to train harder and aim for more wins. The cycle continues—it's a fulfilling loop where motivation and success feed off each other.

As young athletes, it's vital to focus on these small yet substantial psychological benefits of celebrating. By acknowledging your triumphs, no matter how minor, you're actively engaging in building a stronger, more positive version of yourself. This is especially meaningful in competitive sports like softball, where mental strength often dictates performance outcomes. Positive reinforcements through celebrations make all the difference in strengthening your self-belief for both present challenges and future ones.

Create a Visual Reminder of Your Accomplishments

Creating reminders of your successes is a powerful way to boost your confidence and motivation, especially when you're looking to strengthen your mental game. One effective method to achieve this is through the use of visual accomplishment boards to serve as a continuous source of personalized inspiration.

Visual Accomplishment Boards

Visual accomplishment boards are essentially collages of images, words, and symbols that represent your goals, achievements, and personal growth. By displaying them prominently in your room or workspace, they act as daily reminders of what you have achieved and what you aspire to become. This constant visibility can increase your motivation by keeping your goals at the forefront of your mind, urging you to push yourself further each day.

To make these boards more meaningful, it's essential to incorporate a variety of elements. Photos from games or tournaments where you've excelled can remind you of those triumphant moments. Awards or recognitions, whether they're certificates or small trophies, also serve as acknowledgments of your hard work and dedication. Including quotes from athletes you admire or from motivational speakers can give you that extra push when you're feeling less enthusiastic. The different types of content keep the board from getting boring, so it continues to captivate and inspire you every time you look at it.

Routine Reflection on Visuals

Routine reflection on your visual accomplishment board is crucial for reinforcing a winning mindset. Taking a few minutes each day to review the board while thinking about the emotions tied to those achievements and aspirations helps build a resilient mindset. This practice not only feeds your drive to succeed but also nurtures gratitude for how far you've come.

Sharing Achievements

Sharing your accomplishments through visual reminders can create a sense of community support and encourage recognition among peers. By inviting friends or teammates to view your board, you open up opportunities for mutual encouragement and collaboration. Discussing each other's goals and victories can lead to shared insights and strategies, strengthening team bonds and building a supportive network. This communal aspect emphasizes the importance of recognizing not just individual success but also collective progress within your team or peer group.

The process of creating and maintaining a visual accomplishment board is an empowering exercise that combines creativity with introspection. Before starting, take time to reflect on what you truly want to accomplish in different areas of your life. Set clear intentions and be specific about your goals. For instance, if improving your batting average is a goal, include visuals related to that, like pictures of successful swings or statistics showing your progress. Use positive affirmations to bolster your belief in your abilities, such as "I am capable of achieving my dreams" or "I have the strength and focus to excel."

Exercise: Creating Your Visual Accomplishment Board

Objective: To help you develop a visual reminder board that serves as a source of motivation, inspiration, and community support.

Part 1: Introduction to Visual Accomplishment Boards

- **What is a Visual Board?**

  - A visual accomplishment board is a creative space where you can display reminders of your achievements, goals, and inspirations. This board can help you stay motivated, especially during challenging times.

- **Creating Your Space:**

  - Find a place in your room or locker where you can display your visual board. It could be a corkboard, poster board, or even digital (using apps or platforms you prefer).

Part 2: Incorporating Various Elements

- **What to include:**

  - **Photos:** Include pictures of yourself in action, with teammates, or at events. You might also include images of athletes you admire.

  - **Awards and achievements:** Display any medals, certificates, or notes of accomplishment that reflect your hard work.

  - **Quotes and mantras:** Write down motivational quotes or personal affirmations. Examples:

    - "I am strong, I am fierce, and I can achieve anything I set my mind to!"

    - "Every challenge is an opportunity for growth."

- **Customize your board:**

  - Reflect on what personal values and aspirations are most important to you. Include items that represent those values, such as symbols of teamwork, perseverance, or dedication.

- **Collaborate with teammates:**

○ Host a board-making session with your teammates. Share accomplishments, photos, and quotes, and encourage each other by showcasing everyone's successes.

Part 3: Routine Reflection on Visuals

- **Regular revisits:**

  ○ Set a routine to review your visual board weekly. Spend a few minutes looking at each element and reflecting on its significance.

  ○ Ask yourself:

    ■ What accomplishment am I most proud of?

    ■ How can I use this reminder to overcome challenges I'm facing?

- **Daily ritual:**

  ○ Incorporate your visual board into your daily routine. Whether it's a morning motivation boost or a pre-practice pep talk, spend time absorbing the positivity you've created.

- **Practice gratitude:**

  ○ Each week, in your journal, write down one thing you're grateful for regarding your journey in softball. This encourages a positive mindset and reminds you of your progress.

Part 4: Sharing Achievements

- **Community support:**

  ○ Share your visual accomplishment board with your teammates, coach, or family. Create a supportive environment where everyone feels encouraged to celebrate their own and each other's successes.

- **Promote celebration:**

- Organize team sessions where each player shares a highlight from their visual board. Recognizing accomplishments fosters a culture of celebration and helps everyone feel valued.

- **Encouragement and inspiration:**

    - Encourage your teammates to recognize their achievements. Create a shared space where you can collectively celebrate personal milestones, whether through a group chat or regular team meetings.

Reflection

At the end of the season or a significant period, look back at your visual accomplishment board and reflect on:

- How did your board help you stay motivated?

_____
_____
_____
_____
_____
_____
_____
_____
_____
_____
_____
_____

- What were the highlights of your journey that stood out?

_____
_____
_____
_____
_____
_____
_____
_____
_____
_____
_____
_____

- How did sharing your accomplishments with others enhance your experience?

_____
_____
_____
_____
_____
_____
_____
_____
_____
_____
_____

_____

By creating and regularly engaging with a visual accomplishment board, you'll cultivate motivation, celebrate your journey, and inspire those around you—making your softball experience even more fulfilling!

Bringing It Home

In this chapter, we dove into how recognizing both big and small achievements can really pump up your confidence and motivation. Understanding that each little win counts builds a positive mindset, making you feel more sure of yourself in sports like softball. We talked about keeping a success log to track these victories and learned how celebrating milestones, even with something as simple as a high-five or team huddle, brings everyone closer and boosts morale. It's all about seeing the progress you've made and using those moments to fuel your journey forward.

The idea is to create habits and rituals that make celebrating achievements natural and fun. By setting up personal reminders of your successes, like visual boards or logs, you're constantly reminded of what you've accomplished and motivated to keep going. This practice not only helps improve your performance on the field but also teaches you how to tackle life's ups and downs with resilience. Remember, it's about enjoying the ride, appreciating every effort, and learning from each step forward. Keep celebrating those wins, and you'll find confidence growing inside you, ready for whatever challenge comes next!

Conclusion

As you close this book, remember what you've learned here is just the beginning. You're stepping onto a path that not only strengthens your softball game but also lights up other areas of your life. You've got the tools, techniques, and insights to build an unbreakable mental game, making your time on—and off—the field richer and more rewarding.

Every time you face a challenge or doubt yourself, you're now equipped with ways to handle those moments. It's like having a secret weapon. Whether it's harnessing your nervous energy into excitement, bouncing back from setbacks stronger than ever, or confidently trusting in your abilities, you've set yourself up for success. Your journey won't always be easy, but with a positive mindset, you're already halfway there. Embrace every challenge as a chance to improve, and you'll surpass what you once thought were your limits.

Believing in yourself and your abilities is where it all starts. Confidence doesn't just happen overnight; it grows when you recognize your strengths and achievements. Celebrate every little win and use them as stepping stones to build even more confidence. Remember, positive self-talk can change how you approach everything. Instead of fearing mistakes, view them as opportunities to learn and grow. When your self-doubt kicks in, remind yourself of how far you've come and all the incredible things you're capable of achieving.

Mistakes are part of the game, and they don't define you. What really matters is how you respond to them. Those who bounce back and keep moving forward after setbacks become resilient. If you welcome this mindset, you'll understand that setbacks are normal and help you reach greater things. Each stumble is a chance to become stronger and wiser for the next competition. Remember, mistakes don't mark the end—they're merely chapters in your ongoing story of strength and persistence.

Another key aspect of building a strong mental game is understanding the importance of the community around you. Being part of a team offers unique support that individual achievements can't match. A successful team thrives on trust and open communication. When you and your teammates encourage each other, everyone benefits. By working together, you create a positive environment that amplifies each player's potential. No one succeeds alone, and the unity within a team allows for both collective and personal growth. Everyone's success feeds the group's strength and unity, creating a powerful synergy that boosts performance and camaraderie.

As you wrap up this book, I encourage you to revisit the exercises whenever you need that extra push or when you feel stuck. They're designed to be your go-to resource, helping you practice and fine-tune your mental skills at your own pace. Feel free to take your time—it's not about rushing through them but about truly absorbing the lessons they offer. You might find that some exercises resonate more with you at different points in your life, so keep coming back to them. Use them as a toolkit you can dip into whenever you need guidance or a boost.

This book isn't just about playing better softball or winning more games; it's about empowering yourself with a mindset that will carry you through many aspects of life. These skills will help you handle pressure, adapt to new challenges, and lead a more confident and fulfilling life beyond the sports field. The mental toughness and resilience you build here will stay with you no matter where life takes you. So, continue to strengthen these skills and make them a natural part of your daily routine to stay prepared for whatever comes your way.

Building a solid mental foundation is a lifelong process that involves dedication and self-reflection. Keep setting goals and tracking your progress, learning from every experience along the way. Never stop pushing yourself to improve, and know that each step forward, no matter how small, is significant. With perseverance and determination, you'll continue to grow and achieve things beyond your imagination.

As you finish this chapter of growth, consider sharing your journey with others. Your experience and insights could inspire fellow athletes to work on their mental game, too. By writing a review, you help spread the word to those looking to strengthen their performance and boost their confidence. Together, we can empower more young female athletes to reach their full potential, both on the field and in life. Your voice matters and has the power to influence and uplift others who are embarking on the same path. Thank you for taking this journey, and remember—you've got the power to achieve amazing things!

Thank You!

I want to take a moment to personally thank you for picking up *The Mental Side of Softball for Young Female Athletes*. Your dedication to strengthening your mindset is what sets you apart, and I hope this book has given you the tools to build confidence, focus, and resilience on and off the field.

Softball is just as much mental as it is physical, and by training your mind, you're giving yourself an edge that separates good players from great ones. Keep believing in yourself, trusting your process, and embracing every challenge as an opportunity to grow.

Leave a Review!

Your feedback means the world to me, and it helps other athletes find this book. If *The Mental Side of Softball for Young Female Athletes* has made an impact on your game, I'd love to hear your thoughts!

➔📱 **Scan the QR code below** to leave a quick review—it only takes a minute and makes a huge difference.

Thank you again for being part of this journey. Keep playing with confidence, and remember— the strongest players are the ones who trust their mindset just as much as their mechanics!

See you on the field,
Vicky McFarland

References

Adams, A. J. (2020). Seeing is believing: The power of visualization. *Psychology Today.* https://www.psychologytoday.com/ca/blog/flourish/200912/seeing-is-believing-the-power-visualization

Bailey, J. R., & Rehman, S. (2022, March 4). *Don't underestimate the power of self-reflection.* Harvard Business Review; Harvard Business Review. https://hbr.org/2022/03/dont-underestimate-the-power-of-self-reflection

Broadway, K. (2023, May 25). The benefits of mindfulness for student-athletes. *NCSA Sports.* https://www.ncsasports.org/blog/benefits-of-mindfulness-for-athletes

Carter, L. (2023, March 21). *How does a certified sports psychology coach help an athlete with distraction control?* Spencer Institute Health, Holistic and Wellness Certifications. https://spencerinstitute.com/how-does-a-certified-sports-psychology-coach-help-an-athlete-with-distraction-control/

Cascio, C. N., O'Donnell, M. B., Tinney, F. J., Lieberman, M. D., Taylor, S. E., Strecher, V. J., & Falk, E. B. (2015). Self-affirmation activates brain systems associated with self-related processing and reward and is reinforced by future orientation. *Social Cognitive and Affective Neuroscience, 11*(4), 621–629. https://doi.org/10.1093/scan/nsv136

Cherry, K. (2023, August 14). *7 useful tips for improving your mental focus.* Verywell Mind. https://www.verywellmind.com/things-you-can-do-to-improve-your-mental-focus-4115389

Cherry, K. (2024, June 25). *Self efficacy: Why believing in yourself matters.* Verywell Mind. https://www.verywellmind.com/what-is-self-efficacy-2795954

Cleere, M. (2018, May 2). The impact of body language on performance. *Dr. Michelle Cleere.* https://drmichellecleere.com/blog/impact-body-language-performance/

Concentration and attention. (2024). Virginia Tech Athletics. https://hokiesports.com/concentration-and-attention

Constructive criticism tips for young athletes. (n.d.). *Youthsportspsychology.* https://www.youthsportspsychology.com/youth_sports_psychology_blog/constructive-criticism-tips-for-young-athletes/

Coutinho, M. (2018, November 23). *The role of mental toughness in sport performance.* Elite FTS. https://www.elitefts.com/education/the-role-of-mental-toughness-in-sport-

performance/?srsltid=AfmBOopBnYuGxMTYD7RP5teETem6_MnPgfpgDLr1ZvQC7t7h
vr_PLzFZ

Crim, J. (2023a, May 30). *How to develop the power of visualization in sports performance.* THE BEHAVIOUR INSTITUTE. https://thebehaviourinstitute.com/how-to-develop-the-power-of-visualization-in-sports-performance/

Crim, J. (2023b, May 31). *Sports psychology exercises for concentration and focus.* Behaviour Institute. https://thebehaviourinstitute.com/sports-psychology-exercises-to-improve-your-concentration-and-focus/

Crimmins, J. (2023, May 30). *Goal-Setting secrets in sports psychology.* Behaviour Institute. https://thebehaviourinstitute.com/maximizing-performance-uncover-goal-setting-secrets-in-sports-psychology/

Dailyhuman. (2024, April 8). *The mental game: Key strategies for athletes' mental preparation.* Dailyhuman. https://www.dailyhuman.com/post/athletes-mental-preparation

Drummond, J. (2023, November 20). 7 tips to help athletes improve their mental health. *Jenn Drummond.* https://jenndrummond.com/blog/7-tips-to-help-athletes-improve-their-mental-health/

Endo, T., Sekiya, H., & Chiaki Raima. (2023). Psychological pressure on athletes during matches and practices. *Asian Journal of Sport and Exercise Psychology, 3*(3). https://doi.org/10.1016/j.ajsep.2023.07.002

Finch, J. (n.d.). *Jennie Finch quotes.* BrainyQuote. https://www.brainyquote.com/authors/jennie-finch-quotes

Foster, L. (2023, May 8). *Mental strategies for athletic performance: Unleash full potential.* Educate Fitness. https://educatefitness.co.uk/mental-strategies-for-athletic-performance-unleash-your-full-potential/

Gail, C. (2023). Team communication: Effective group collaboration & teamwork. *Crystal.* https://www.crystalknows.com/blog/team-communication

Gupta, S., & McCarthy, P. (2022). The sporting resilience model: A systematic review of resilience in sport performers. *Frontiers in Psychology, 13*(1). https://doi.org/10.3389/fpsyg.2022.1003053

Jekauc, D., Fiedler, J., Wunsch, K., Mülberger, L., Burkart, D., Kilgus, A., & Fritsch, J. (2023). The effect of self-confidence on performance in sports: a meta-analysis and narrative review. *International Review of Sport and Exercise Psychology*, 1–27. https://doi.org/10.1080/1750984x.2023.2222376

Jonov, C. (2023, January 23). *Taking the reins: The powerful effects of accountability.* Medium. https://medium.com/@colin.jonov10/taking-the-reins-the-powerful-effects-of-accountability-44fd7ee6af2

Karageorghis, C. (n.d.). *Motivation in sports psychology.* Sports Performance Bulletin. https://www.sportsperformancebulletin.com/psychology/coping-with-emotions/motivation-in-sports-psychology

Lanquist, L. (2017, October 18). *17 athletes who'll inspire you to love your damn self.* SELF. https://www.self.com/gallery/body-positive-athletes

Lochbaum, M., Sherburn, M., Sisneros, C., Cooper, S., Lane, A. M., & Terry, P. C. (2022). Revisiting the self-confidence and sport performance relationship: A systematic review with meta-analysis. *International Journal of Environmental Research and Public Health*, *19*(11), 6381. https://doi.org/10.3390/ijerph19116381

Lovering, N. (2022, May 9). *Neuroplasticity and childhood trauma: Effects, healing, and EMDR.* Psych Central. https://psychcentral.com/ptsd/the-roles-neuroplasticity-and-emdr-play-in-healing-from-childhood-trauma

McCoy, J. (2020, March 31). *40 most powerful women athletes of all time.* Glamour. https://www.glamour.com/story/most-powerful-female-athletes-of-all-time

Medinabasketball. (2024, January 29). *A guide to crafting a winning team culture for coaches and players.* Medium. https://medium.com/@team.medinabasketball/a-guide-to-crafting-a-winning-team-culture-for-coaches-and-players-401405194df7

Mental training for athletes: Mindfulness for peak performance. (2024, May 3). *Scorability.* https://www.scorability.com/blog/mental-training-for-athletes/

Moore, C. (2019, March 4). *Positive daily affirmations: Is there science behind it?* Positive Psychology. https://positivepsychology.com/daily-affirmations/

Murphy, D. (2024, June 7). *Posture and how it affects your health | brown university health.* Brown University Health. https://www.brownhealth.org/be-well/posture-and-how-it-affects-your-health

Nortje, A. (2020, July 1). *10+ best grounding techniques and exercises to strengthen your mindfulness practice today.* PositivePsychology.com. https://positivepsychology.com/grounding-techniques/

Nuetzel, B. (2023). Coping strategies for handling stress and providing mental health in elite athletes: A systematic review. *Frontiers in Sports and Active Living*, *5*(1). https://doi.org/10.3389/fspor.2023.1265783

Park, I., & Jeon, J. (2023). Psychological skills training for athletes in sports: Web of science bibliometric analysis. *Healthcare*, *11*(2), 259. https://doi.org/10.3390/healthcare11020259

Park, S.-H., Lim, B.-S., & Lim, S.-T. (2020). The effects of self-talk on shooting athletes' motivation. *Journal of Sports Science & Medicine*, *19*(3), 517. https://pmc.ncbi.nlm.nih.gov/articles/PMC7429435/

Puentes, J. P. (2024, March 13). *Visualization techniques and mental imagery for athletes.* Performance Psych. https://www.performancepsychologycenter.com/post/visualization-techniques-and-mental-imagery

Reinebo, G., Alfonsson, S., Jansson-Fröjmark, M., Rozental, A., & Lundgren, T. (2023). Effects of psychological interventions to enhance athletic performance: A systematic review and meta-analysis. *Sports Medicine*, *54*. https://doi.org/10.1007/s40279-023-01931-z

The relationship between self-confidence and performance. (2023). Www.trine.edu. https://www.trine.edu/academics/centers/center-for-sports-studies/blog/2023/the_relationship_between_self-confidence_and_performance.aspx

Richardson, M. (2023, October 19). *The power of positive psychology: Building resilience in young athletes.* Legacy pro Sports. https://legacyprosports.us/the-power-of-positive-psychology-building-resilience-in-young-athletes/

Roychowdhury, D. (2023, May 28). *The power of visualization: Enhancing performance in sport and exercise.* Dr Dev Roychowdhury. https://www.drdevroy.com/visualization-in-sport-and-exercise/

Shimits, A. (2024, June 29). *Unlocking peak performance: A performance psychology specialist's guide to improving mental toughness.* Persistencepsych.com. https://www.persistencepsych.com/unlocking-peak-performance-a-performance-psychology-specialists-guide-to-improving-mental-toughness

Sievers, C. (2016, December 1). *63 softball quotes we love.* Www.flosoftball.com. https://www.flosoftball.com/articles/5058336-63-softball-quotes-we-love

Stibich, M. (2024, January 1). *How to make your health goals S.M.A.R.T.* Verywell Mind. https://www.verywellmind.com/smart-goals-for-lifestyle-change-2224097

Straw, E. (2023, November 10). *Fixed vs growth mindset in sports*. Success Starts Within. https://www.successstartswithin.com/sports-psychology-articles/athlete-mental-training/fixed-vs-growth-mindset-in-sports/

Sutelan, E. (2024, August 13). *Where is Mo'ne Davis now? Little league world series legend working to become a broadcaster*. Sportingnews.com. https://www.sportingnews.com/ca/mlb/news/mone-davis-little-league-world-series/1k12um9z8gib011m94x5snjnx0

Taubenfeld, E. (2024, October 1). *76 motivational sports quotes for success on and off the field*. Reader's Digest. https://www.rd.com/article/sports-quotes/

Taylor, J. (2023, February 9). Smiling is a powerful mental tool for endurance athletes. *Psychology Today*. https://www.psychologytoday.com/ca/blog/the-power-of-prime/202302/smiling-is-a-powerful-mental-tool-for-endurance-athletes

10 inspiring examples of highly resilient sportspeople. (n.d.). *Resiliencei.com*. https://resiliencei.com/blog/10-inspiring-examples-of-highly-resilient-sportspeople

Walia, B. (2024, October 24). *Rediscovering the power of self-belief*. BPS; The British Psychological Society. https://www.bps.org.uk/psychologist/rediscovering-power-self-belief

Zotey, V., Andhale, A., Shegekar, T., & Juganavar, A. (2023). Adaptive neuroplasticity in brain injury recovery: Strategies and insights. *Cureus*, *15*(9). https://doi.org/10.7759/cureus.45873

Made in United States
Orlando, FL
14 April 2025